Te:

The story John tells in thes
his experience alive and sheds light on being gay, surviving
cancer, and learning to cherish the small blessings of life.
Definitely worth the read.
**~ Rev. James Brandt, Ph.D., Professor of Historical Theology,
Saint Paul School of Theology and Singer, Heartland Men's
Chorus**

I personally know John and I have to say that he is quite a
remarkable man. The depth of adversity he faced in his story
and what he overcame speaks volumes about his character
and legacy. Just the first two chapters of Johns book makes
you never want to set it down. His story has a way of making
you want to appreciate life ever so deeply. I experience myself
as moved by his story and honored to call him my friend. Love
you John.
~ Allen Little, TEDx Speaker & Life Coach

Being diagnosed with cancer is daunting, but John shows us
how to use our challenges to strip away the excess noise,
getting to the root of our true, higher selves. Retracing the
steps of his personal journey helped me to mine the gifts that
cancer has given me—hope, love, and the peace that passes all
understanding. Whether you or a family member is newly
diagnosed, in the midst of the battle, or even in remission—
this book is a must-read.
**~ Elly Brown, oral cancer survivor and social media
influencer**

John takes us through his life experiences with love, appreciation and a warm authentic sense of humor that will make you laugh out loud. His writing lets us see the beauty and the gifts on his journey of healing.
~ Virginia Firestone RScP, Licensed Science of Mind Practitioner and Visioning Facilitator

Well-written and an easy read. An honest story of growing up in a rural area. A testimony of attending church establishing strong faith that served him well in dealing with and being healed of cancer, John D. is a man of deep faith.
~ Bill Hodges, Longtime Friend and Spiritual Seeker

Upon reading John's words, my heart began to smile. There were so many parts of his life that I could relate and identify with in regard to small town, family dynamics and love. I have been blessed to know just a glimmer of John's life and struggle but will never forget the night that he shared with the Heartland Men's Chorus the miracle that had happened in his life. This book is a journey of a lifetime that shares the strength, joy, and grace of a man of faith. John is a man who gives as much of himself as he can to encourage and love not only his biological family, but his family of choice. This is truly a testament to a good and faithful servant of God.
~ Presten Fry, Director of Traditional Music at Christ United Methodist Church, Independence, MO

John describes his coming of age and coming out in a creative and descriptive way. He loved the flowers, the gardening, and he loved making things pretty. He was sensitive, and felt in his heart he was different, and something was wrong. As he explores his genesis and ultimately his coming out, John describes farm life and his family in a way that is familiar to anyone who has ever lived in small-town America. His experience is unique, and he is a wonderful storyteller.
~ Julia Thomas, Member of Center for Spiritual Living Kansas City

John Delameter invites us to "jump in" and ride along as he travels through the experiences that have shaped his life. The view is spectacular in its raw, uncensored honesty. He doesn't detour around his fear in facing challenging circumstances and choices. It's a must-read look at a life lived with courage and conviction—lovingly set with the scenic backdrop of his small-town roots. Sit back and enjoy the ride.
~ Jeanne Looper Smith, Motivational Speaker, and author of *Retro Road Trip: Taking the Long Way Home*

I enjoyed reading the chapters and the way John described his life growing up. It reminded me of stories my grandmother used to tell me about life in rural Kansas on the farm. The stories are vivid and insightful about life in a small town in a big family. I liked the wholesomeness and simplicity [and] enjoyed every moment of what I read.
~ Thomas Alonzo, LGBTQ activist

I love the way John takes everyday things and gives me insight into our natures and courage to keep "planting blubs" even though we may not see them bloom.
~ Josh Farrell, Friend

John has a way of writing that makes me feel like I am right there, watching him plant his tulips. His sense of humor in such a trying time of his life is refreshing. His faith in himself, and the creator is remarkable. We would all benefit from taking notes and live our lives with a touch of his armor! His attitude is contagious.
~ Cheryl Wyrick, Longtime Friend and Fellow Gardener

I have a Brother of the heart in John Delameter and have loved and adored him for many years. He is truly a wonderful person who would do anything for a friend. I am so proud that he has done what he told me many years ago that he was going to do - write a book about his life. I believe we were in dirt, elbow deep, in one of my flower beds planting bulbs at the time. His story reads like John talks: with subtle humor, in plain, easy to understand language with no frills (pun intended)! It brings back memories of an Americana time of life, when things were so much simpler. I am sure when this book is complete, it will be loved and appreciated by those who know John, and especially by those who will be introduced to him and blessed by his story for the first time. I Remain his Sister in Christ.
~ Lisa Park, member of Spirit of Hope, Kansas City's Metropolitan Community Church

I Dedicate this Book to Richard Fawcett

This dedication, in many ways, was almost the hardest thing for me to write.

What do you say to or about someone who helped transform your life—a life overflowing with decades-old childhood stories about feelings of unworthiness, not being wanted, not fitting in, and being completely unlovable—to one of authenticity, self-love, openness, gratitude, purpose, acceptance, and so much more?

How do you properly thank someone for revealing to you a life filled with the Spirit of God and a connection to the oneness that we all came here to be, to a life that I felt worthy of living?

"Thank you" seems so insufficient.

As I say later in the book, Richard Fawcett turned out to be one of the greatest teachers my soul has ever known, leading me down paths I didn't even know existed that not only saved my life but completely transformed it.

Spiritually led, intuitive, open, willing, knowledgeable, level-headed, committed, understanding, trustworthy, respectful … these are just a few of the many words I use to describe him.

Again, words that feel so inadequate.

Richard, I love and dedicate this book to you because you taught me how to raise my vibration and focus my thoughts on life, not death.

You showed me, by example, the importance of meditation and the language we use when speaking about ourselves, our circumstances, and others.

You assumed a strong, never-flinching personal and professional interest in my spiritual growth, sharing yours along the way as well.

You taught me that by always keeping my guard up in an attempt to keep the hurtful things out, I was also preventing anything and anyone good, healthy, beautiful, and just what my soul needed, from getting in.

You shared with me so many inspiring quotes from a wide variety of religious and spiritual scholars and teachers – words that helped me at my lowest and continue to feed me in my current knowing of myself.

You offered great wisdom through the work of Dr. George Goodheart and muscle testing, as well as that of Dr. Bradley Nelson and his *Emotion Code* book and chart. Through you— and them—I learned to listen to my body because, as you always say, "The body doesn't lie. It cannot lie."

You loved me through every step of the cancer journey and never—not once—tried to steer me away from traditional medicine or procedures to address the cancer that had invaded my vital organs. Instead, you pointed out that if I were willing, I could try another way. I could use my own body and mental outlook to heal.

There are no guarantees, you said, "But you don't have to accept this condition as a death sentence. You can be the exception."

The man that I am today is wide open, loveable, worthy, attractive, giving, vulnerable, willing, happy, healthy, whole, and completely transformed—mind, body, and spirit.

Although you'd probably say that it was me—not you—who did the work (and boy was it hard work!), I stand firm in giving you so much of the glory and praise for what you have done. For those who don't necessarily believe in angels, I have to tell you that Richard truly is one.

I still don't have an answer for why tapping into my Divine Essence and inner knowing saved me from departing my physical body eight years ago, and why others met their demise, and crossed over to the other side.

Yet I'm alive today as an exception, and what I hope will be an example to others to trust in their Higher Power and know that everything is always, even if we don't understand or want to accept it, in Divine Order.

This student was eventually ready for the teacher who had appeared.

And I will forever remember your words, Richard, when it seemed like all was lost:

"But we also know something."

Introduction

We need to learn to color outside the lines.

We live in a status quo society that says, "This is how we've always done it. This is how we are supposed to do it."

And we've been duped.

We believe that this—whatever that is—is "the way it's supposed to be." But what I've learned in my 77 years of life is that's not always the case, and not always true.

The motto of the United Negro College Fund is, "A Mind is a Terrible Thing to Waste." And they are right. I think there is so much of our minds that we don't use.

Now before we get started, I want everyone to know that I've put very careful thought and consideration into how to share my life path without disrespecting anyone else's. Yet I know that a great deal of it intersects with the personal life of others – namely my family members.

It's sometimes a very delicate and fine line between trying not to make other people upset, and living my truth—completely, authentically, and without regrets.

Within these pages is a lot of, as the saying goes, "The good, the bad, and the ugly." You may be shocked, embarrassed, angry, or even hurt by some of the things I've said and done—way back when, and now. But I'm also sure that some of it will make you laugh and cry tears of joy.

I would only ask that you please try to understand that everything that has happened in my life has brought me to this point. I know it sounds like a cliché—and at the time I would never have said this—but looking back now I can honestly say I wouldn't have it any other way. **ALL OF IT** has led me to my highest and greatest good.

You may see a lot of yourself and your life path within my story, in which case I hope my words are helpful. If you are struggling, feel hopeless, or want to give up, just know that there are many lessons and blessings in what you're going through, and there is a good life beyond all of that.

I believe that God brought me through all of this because in some way the world still needs me, and it needs you too.

I also believe that we have a Power and Presence within us that can change whatever we need to change. And I did. Not just my mind, but my heart, my faith, my beliefs, my energy, and yes, my life.

Now, I'm not a doctor and would never tell someone not to seek out a medical professional. So please don't misunderstand what I'm saying to mean that we can cure any physical ailment with only positive thoughts. However, we can *always* give positive healing energy to it.

Despite the medical prognosis, that's exactly what I did - focused on positive healing energy.

It certainly could have ended the way they said. But it didn't.

This is my story.

"For I know the plans that I have for you," declares the Lord, "plans for welfare and not for calamity to give you a future and a hope."

Jeremiah 29:11
(New American Standard Bible Version)

My Story

Chapter 1
<u>Planting Bulbs in March</u>

It was beautiful although slightly chilly day in Kansas City, KS on what turned out to be anything but an ordinary day.

It was March 2012, and I was out in my garden planting flower bulbs that would bloom at the start of spring a few weeks later.

Gardening has always been one of my favorite hobbies – a circle of life process of planting something that would grow out of sight deep in the earth for a while, later making a grand entrance in a burst of brilliant colors.

It's something I learned growing up on a farm where my parents grew corn, soybeans, hay, and other foodstuffs, along with raising livestock, cows, pigs, sheep, and 11 kids! "Homegrown labor" was an essential part of the formula, after all.

As a young boy I remember my dad and older brothers working the bottom land of our family property, planting all of these crops with great expectation of the bounty they would yield. A good harvest was about 25 percent of our income, or a loss in equal measure if the Midwest rains proved too much that year.

Dad was always big on diversifying. His concern was, if we planted everything in, say, corn, and we had a bad year, then we'd have nothing. He was always thinking ahead. We never got rich, but we always had what we needed.

An uncle planted soybeans one year and they "hit," so much so that he was later able to retire and move to Florida! So, I guess playing farm crop roulette could pay big dividends if the wheel stopped at just the right place. But if it hadn't worked, his kids would probably still be paying off the family farm.

On this particular day it was just me and Mother Earth, working side-by-side, playing our part in this annual circle of life ritual that brought so much beauty to my garden and my life.

Now if you have even a little bit of a green thumb and are familiar with living in the Midwest you might be thinking right about now, "Why is he planting bulbs in March?" That's a fair question!

I had gone to the Kansas City Remodel + Garden Show just a few weeks before and found these cute little frozen tulip and daffodil bulbs. Like me, most people buy and plant them in the fall, but the pictures on the packages were so beautiful, I just had to have some more to satisfy my spring fever cravings! So until the time was right, I re-stashed them in the freezer next to my carton of Ben and Jerry's ice cream! And I knew that if planted at just the right moment they would make my yard look so beautiful.

During a short break inside the house to get a cup of coffee, my cell phone rang. I wasn't at all surprised to see my doctor's phone number on the caller ID, as I'd just been to his office a week or so ago for a check-up and some blood work.

Years later when people ask me about that call, the best way I can describe what he said was the sound it would have made if somebody dumped a large case of glass marbles down a concrete stairway. For me that crashing sound was accompanied by unthinkable words:

Stage 4 Cancer.

     Inoperable.

          Incurable.

               Terminal.

                    Irreparable.

                    Fatal.

                        Lethal.

     Six-to-eight months to live.

I'm so sorry, John.

My brain couldn't make any sense of it at the time. Suddenly, that crashing sound and those words were just there.

It took a few hours before my brain could send me any kind of understandable communication. What did get through was devastating:

"That call was for me."

"It was *my* number the doctor dialed - not a co-worker, or a family member, or my neighbor. He called me."

"It was real."

"It did happen."

When finally able to move, I called my friend, Bill Hodges, who lived about 25 minutes away in Independence, MO. He and I had met in the early '80s in a 12-step recovery group and had been friends ever since.

Ours was the kind of naturally flowing friendship where when he got paid, I'd go over to see him and we'd go to the lumber yard or hardware store and buy something to fix his house. The next week when I got paid, we did the reverse. If he found some helpful quote or something good for people in recovery, he'd share it with me, and vice versa. Over the years, we joked that we'd done everything together except *that!*

Like always when answering the phone, Bill said in his fun-loving way, "Hey, what's going on?"

"Well, I just got a call from the doctor," I replied, with a cracking voice.

"What did he say?"

"It's not good. 'Inoperable and incurable cancer' he said. I've been given six to eight months to live."

Looking back, I think maybe Bill had some marbles crashing in his ears as well, not uttering a word while he tried to process what I'd just said.

After a long silence he finally responded. "I'll be right there."

When he arrived, I was back out in the garden, digging carefully placed holes, approximately six inches apart, for my beautiful bulbs. I was making every attempt to arrange them in other than straight symmetrical rows so when they flowered, they would look like nature had organized them. As I was doing so, it was starting to sink in that I may not be around to see them bloom after all.

Bill just stood there, looking at me; me looking at him.

Finally, I said, "Well, we've gone through a lot of things together, but I never thought about this day."

Chapter 2
<u>Princeton, Missouri</u>

I was born in 1943 and grew up in Princeton, MO, the county seat of Mercer County.

Located in the far north central part of the state just south of the Iowa border, Princeton's claim to fame is as the birthplace in 1852 of Martha Jane Cannary (or Canary, according to some historical records) Burke, better known as Calamity Jane.

Known for her Wild West-era capers (she ran with the likes of Wild Bill Hickok and his gang), whiskey drinkin', quick wit and tongue, and amazing sharp-shooting skills, she was also well-loved for her charitable works and kindness and love for others.

Who she was is a lot like some of the people who lived in my beloved Princeton, a little town of about 1,100 people when I was growing up: gentle, compassionate, good ole boys and girls who were always there for you. Yet they also had a fiery side, full of rambunctious Saturday night beer drinkers and self-appointed renegades, who could terrify (mostly harmlessly) the streets with the best of 'em!

Everyone in my family was very head and heart strong too, tackling their own unexpected life challenges with an admirable determination to "make this work."

A sister who'd made close friends with the bottle eventually chose a world of sobriety, creating a new life that was real and fulfilling.

Another sister who had smoked for over three decades, including several unsuccessful attempts at quitting, eventually stopped cold turkey after seeing a look of sheer terror on her son's face when severe breathing issues earned her an ambulance ride to the hospital. It wasn't until years later that I learned my marble-dropping diagnosis was the thing that really encouraged her to stick with it. She'd had a chance at life, she said, but at that time it looked like I would not. Remaining smoke-free was a struggle she was willing to take on in my honor (Thank you, sister!).

Not long after my doctor called that chilly March day I, too, dug into my Princeton, Delameter, tough guy roots deciding, "No. That's not going to happen!" I would later tell friends and family, "He didn't know who he was talking to!"

Maybe we got this inner strength from our dad. On almost a daily basis during the rainy season when we were growing up, he walked from our farmhouse (where he was also born and raised) about a quarter mile up a slight hill, gazing down on the other side at the bottom land crops after a really heavy rain to see if the river had overflowed its banks and washed away everything we'd planted. Watching him from the house, just standing there for quite a while looking around, I kind of figured, "OK, the crops are gone."

When he came back humming or singing my mother was the first to ask, "Well?" And he'd say, "Well, it's out (referring to the times the river had jumped its banks). It's clear up to 'such and such.'" And then he'd just go on with whatever he was going to do that day.

His words and actions really stuck with my siblings and me as: *That's gone. I can't change this. Flush it and do something different. Keep moving.*

The "Serenity Prayer" by the great American theologian, Reinhold Niebuhr, shares the same philosophy:

> *God grant me the serenity to accept*
> *the things I cannot change,*
> *courage to change the things I can,*
> *and wisdom to know the difference.*

* * *

I didn't realize how Americana my youth was in Princeton until I moved to the "big city"—Lincoln, NE—in 1962. There, whenever I would talk about drinking soda pops on the square with my friends, Saturday night concerts on the bandstand, marching in our homecoming parades and such, people would always say, "You just had the best childhood!"

Growing up you don't think of it as being "the best childhood." You just go from day-to-day, living life, not really questioning if it was good or bad. It just was.

My early education was at East High Point Elementary, a little one-room country school about three miles from our farmhouse; one of a bunch of little one-room country schools dotted throughout the county where you went from 1st grade (there was no kindergarten back then) through 8th grade.

And these weren't classrooms with a lot of kids like those portrayed in the television show *Little House on the Prairie.* Ours only had eight-to-twelve kids and unless someone moved in or out of your little neck of the woods those kids were your classmates until graduating to the big school in town.

Probably the biggest deal was that we had two outhouses, a definite luxury back then.

Always a sensitive kid, I remember that I didn't like it when any of the older boys would cuss or pick on the teacher and try to make her cry. And I much preferred the calm demeanor of the girls and how they showered me with attention. Nevertheless, these kids were an extension of my family and I loved all of them.

We traded items from our packed lunches, and at recess we ran around together playing Dodge Ball and Annie-Over, where you throw the ball over the school roof to the kids on the other side, then run around the building as fast as you can to see if they caught it or not. We just did all of the things kids who are together for so much of the week would do.

One year for our school play we performed the journey to Bethlehem, and my friends Duane, J.L., and I played the wise men while dressed up in our parents' housecoats with paper crowns on our heads and gifts in our hands. And we sang, "We Three Kings."

My mother helped by making a stage curtain out of a bolt of fabric the PTA had purchased, and my dad added hog rings to the top so it could be easily moved back and forth along the bailing wire, which he also strung. We may have been rednecks, but we were classy rednecks!

Everything in our little neck of the woods was just grand.

But a huge unexpected shift in our idyllic lifestyle came at the end of 6th grade.

It happened when the Princeton political powers-that-be held a big election and decided to consolidate all of the one-room schools and send us country kids to the bigger school in town. The idea was to create a stronger school system overall, but among the country folks this decision did not go over well.

First, there was the "If it ain't broke, don't fix it" perspective. Everyone in our community had gone to those little schools for decades, and if it was good enough for this long, why change it?

Some people were afraid their taxes would go way up, and they wouldn't be able to afford to live there anymore.

Others worried that the youngest among us weren't mentally or socially prepared to join a bigger school yet, instead of at age 13 or 14 with two more years of schooling under our belts. What would that do to us psychologically? How would we adapt? Surely it was way too soon.

My parents were very, very much against the move and so upset about the whole thing - the farmer's kids going to school in town. In an ironic twist my father was on the country school board at that time, always leading the charge for better teachers and increased learning opportunities. But not this! Sending us into town now was unthinkable.

As big decisions like this often do, it created a lot of ill feelings between friends and family as people strongly voiced their opinions for or against the merger. Not helping matters was a decades-old, deep social division between the "Town" and the "Country" kids - "the Bumpkins." It was really part of the normal junior high-age push to establish dominance, but for us it was very hurtful. And I was about to get the added "bonus" of repeating the 6th grade.

My mother had already been pushing hard for years to hold me back a grade because I was dyslexic (which we didn't have a name for until high school) and because of it got poor grades. And it didn't help that our one-room schoolhouse teacher, who was just a little older than a kid herself, didn't understand or know how to deal with a dyslexic student (or rude, adolescent boys!).

Well, even though not in the way she imagined, my mother had finally gotten her wish and I, the only student in my 6th grade "class," would finally be held back at the beginning of the next school year. That meant that everyone—the small-town and city folks—would know about it. The cloud of humiliation hanging over my head was enormous, and I was double-doomed, so I thought, to fail. I'd always had this feeling of being very second-class, so the shame of repeating the 6th grade added bitter icing on the cake.

Despite my uneasiness about what all of this meant, I was excited to ride the shiny yellow school bus into town to Princeton Junior High. It was a new adventure, after all, even if I didn't know what I was getting myself into it.

But it wasn't long before I started feeling like the outcome of the election had taken away the sense of security I'd had at my little one-room safe haven, and that the teachers were somewhat against we country kids.

A lot of the adults thought the teachers were perhaps more focused on what this action could do for their careers, than on how to effectively teach *all* of the kids.

There was enough anger between the two to go around.

Since I already thought I wasn't good enough, and in my mind, I'd failed before, I was certain I would never amount to much of anything.

Looking back all these years later, that merger was the best thing that could have happened to me.

I got to be around other kids who had different lifestyles, had kids my own age in my class, and was exposed to more social interaction.

Instead of a single, one-room schoolhouse teacher, I was now in a building with a variety of them with different teaching styles, education levels, and world perspectives. The more people I met the more social skills I gained. That new, larger environment literally opened me up to a bigger world.

By the time we entered Princeton High School as freshman, the town and country division had pretty much melted away and we were, for the most part, just "classmates" and some of us became life-long friends.

Ever since I was a little boy, I've had a love of music. The first instrument I ever played was an older sister's trombone, and later in the high school band—The Marching Tigers—I played the tuba. Some of my fondest memories are of performing at halftime at the football games, marching in the homecoming parades, and traveling 69 miles "way out of town" to Kirksville, MO to play at the homecoming celebration at Northeast Missouri Teacher's College (now Truman State University).

We performed on our hometown bandstand on Saturday nights, and had winter concerts at school. In the spring we traveled to compete in regional music concerts, often returning home with Blue Ribbon honors.

We were also fortunate to have had a fantastic band director, Mr. Horn (yes, that was his real name!), who was raised in

Mercer County. After going away to college, he came back to Princeton to head up the band program.

Even though Mr. Horn loved us and wanted us to look and sound our best, he wouldn't make it today as a teacher because he was very loud, he shouted, and he threw things! But we loved him, and it was just a delight to be in that band. It was truly one of my greatest joys and the highlight of my high school experience.
At the time I never realized that other towns didn't have this kind of community connection. It just seemed so natural to us.

Looking back now as a grown man, for the most part life in Princeton was great. It really was. Of course, as a teenager you might think you have a rough childhood if you get a pimple, or have to sometimes ride in a dirty car (often because my dad chewed and spit Union Tobacco that got stuck all along the door panels!), or your parents wouldn't let you go into town on a Saturday night (such child abuse!).

And there was the year I wanted that brand spankin' new 1959 Ford Galaxy - black with a red interior, with twin mirrors on the front, twin radio arrows on the back, and chrome fender skirts. In my mind not getting one was rough!

So no, I never got everything I wanted (hiss, hiss!) but I had everything I needed. My parents did a wonderful job raising us and, in reality, we never lacked for anything.

As the saying goes, every child needs a village – a place where the community helps raise the children. And we had that

14

(even though I didn't appreciate Mrs. "So and So" telling my parents what Little Johnny was doing at times. But she probably saved my neck a time or two!).

People I didn't know very well would give me encouragement, and when my parents saw some kid speeding down the road they went and told their parents about it.

If someone experienced a personal tragedy, the community rallied together to help. Mother would organize the wives to cook and bake meals, and my dad, who rarely left the farm, would pull the men together to help with any chores or farm work.
Princeton was, and still is, just that kind of place, offering emotional and personal support at every turn. We don't get a lot of that today; we are so closed off from each other.

Little did I know then just how much I'd need those folks when I thought those bulbs I'd planted that spring might be my last.

Chapter 3
Just short of a (Delameter) Dozen

My birth order—the 9th of 11 kids—also played a significant role in my life.

By the way, my father's middle name was Abraham (Charles Abraham) and as you know from the Bible, Abraham had seven sons, as did my daddy. Born in 1898, he was one of 8 kids and my mom, Opal Kelley, who was born in 1903, was also one of 11 (interesting fact, so was her mother and grandmother!).

H.A. (yes, that is his given name!), my oldest brother by a little over 20 years, was drafted and sent to fight in World War II. He was only 19 years old.

As a father now myself, I understand the feeling of the first child leaving home. For my parents, their first child left home and went to war - and didn't come back for three years.

Before H.A. left, he and his wife, Lenora, conceived. And my parents, all upset about the war and everything, decided that maybe they should have another baby, too. That's how I came into this world.

H.A.'s in-laws also had a little boy while he was gone. So, he came back to the states to another little brother (me), a baby brother-in-law (his wife's, parent's son), and a son of his own.

From his memoirs written decades later, just for family and close friends, I learned a lot about the war and some of the horrible things he saw and experienced being in the thick of it in the South Pacific. From his written recollections I realized that this man over there was *my big brother*, not just an unidentified person among a bunch of guys we had read about in the newspaper or seen in documentaries on TV.

In my opinion, H.A. is truly an American hero, sacrificing several years of his youth for our freedom. Not only do I salute him, but also Lenora, his at the time young son, Ellis, and my parents for this sacrifice in having to do without his physical presence while he was out there protecting our country and our freedom. Once home on American soil he became big on the U.S. flag, raising the red, white, and blue every chance he got.

I've noticed that as I've grown older, I honor him and what we stand for as a nation more by having the flag out. On Memorial Day, the 4th of July, and Veteran's Day you know where I live because I have them all over my yard.

After getting settled back home H.A. did several things, including operating a grocery store, buying a farm, and working in construction. As time went on, he and Lenora played their part in birthing the Boomer generation, adding another son, and later getting pregnant with a daughter. They had already named her Leona Joyce, and it crushed everyone when they went to the hospital expecting a baby and came home to an empty bassinette.

Next on the family tree is George, the first of the two-year gaps that happened between most of the siblings as our branches grew down the line.

George married Lenora's sister, Dorothy, so my two brothers married two sisters! George joined the Navy with the hope of traveling around the world, but he never left the United States. He served in California, came back home, and opened a little service station.

After the birth of the first four of their six children, they sold their property and moved to Lee's Summit, MO. There, George worked at a dairy and for a grain elevator service. Several years later after learning the trade he came up with a better way to run the business and left to establish his own, calling it Delameter Scale Service. The move was a good one and he did very well by it.

My brother Clay, third in the Delameter line, was the Sheriff of Mercer County for three terms, which means that for 12 years of my youth I knew I had to be very careful because big brother was watching!

As Sheriff he lived at the jail which had living quarters for him and his family – his wife Louise, two daughters, and a son. As little kids we always thought that was so neat because when nobody was locked up, we could go in there and look around.

One day, as an adult living in Kansas City, MO I ran across a guy who had lived not far from Princeton. When he learned where I was from, he said, "I used to go over there on Saturday nights, and let me tell you something about that Sheriff over there. He had the biggest hands I had ever seen in my life! Now, he was a good man but, John, he and I had differences of opinion about what a good time was!"

"Did they look like these?" I asked, showing him my hands, to which he answered, "They were about that big, yes."

"Well, you're talking about my big brother!"

We had a big laugh over that one!

Lea (pronounced Lee), the first girl in the family, prides herself on having never lived more than about five miles from her birthplace. Throughout her working years she was an office administrator, the Mercer County courthouse deputy circuit clerk and recorder, and the Princeton deputy city clerk.

She and Loren, her husband, also opened a service station business, working there together, and raised a son. She once told me that gas back then was only 19.9 cents a gallon and for a mere five bucks, she could fill up your entire tank! They later branched out, adding car washes and laundromats.

One of the fondest memories of my youth is when Lea and Loren bought a trailer house. It was 10-feet by 50-feet with all the modern décor—beautiful design touches, turquoise kitchen appliances with matching pots and pans, attractive lighting … everything you would have seen in an upscale magazine of the day. Oh, I thought that was the neatest thing in the whole wide world, and it felt like a palace to me!

"When I get big," I had told them, "I'm going to have me a trailer house just like yours!" Well, by the time I "got big" my taste had changed to older three-story Victorian homes with wraparound porches and balconies. And you just don't find too many trailers with that kind of design!

Now we're down to my brother, Foster, who was always the funny one! He just had this spunky personality and was always good at playing on words. You never knew what he might come up with next!

His family has always remembered the time one of his friends gave him a blow-up doll that he put in the passenger seat of his truck, driving "her" all over conservative Princeton trying to get a reaction out of people. And, oh, did he get it!

During the eulogies at his funeral when he passed, I remember sitting there near his wife, Audrey, and their five children thinking, "Are they talking about me or Foster?" Until that moment, I just didn't realize how close our strange personalities blended together. Even today, I'll hear things from folks from my hometown like, "I knew your brother Foster and, oh, we had a good time! We were always laughing about something!"

Very sweet and very serious about her Baptist faith is one way to describe my sister Lillian. She was the one, since my mother didn't go to church real often and my dad didn't go at all, who made sure her three younger siblings, the last of the Delameter bunch, went to church no matter what! It was a strict rule—or, I guess you could say it was really an unspoken expectation—that we kids had to go to church. No exceptions. Although Lillian moved from Princeton to Trenton about 20 miles south of us where she worked in a bank, she'd come home on the weekends to take us to church Sunday morning and evening, again on Wednesday for the mid-week service, and when it was revival time, every night of the week – for two weeks straight!

After I was old enough to get my driver's license, she moved about an hour and a half southeast to St. Joseph, MO. Many years later I asked, "Did you wait to move away until I got my license so you could be sure we got to church every week?"

"Well, it could be," she slyly replied. I'm convinced that's what the story was, and I give her a lot of credit for making that sacrifice for what she felt was important for us growing up. Lillian later moved to Lincoln, NE, married a man named Ewalt, a widower with a little girl, and together he and Lillian welcomed two boys into their family. They all lived on a farm that had been in his family for a number of years, and their daughter eventually raised her children on that same property.

Next on the family tree is Derald. The real quiet one of the bunch, he had no real plans to leave Princeton until he met and became smitten with this pretty little blonde named Betty, the daughter of a family that had moved from Colorado to a farm next door to ours. When her family moved back to Colorado, it wasn't long before he moved there too. When Betty moved back to Princeton again about a year later, Derald came with her and they eventually got married. Now, after over 50 years of wedded bliss and two children, he still follows that cute little blonde all over town!

Other than a stint in the Army when he was stationed at Fort Hood, TX (at the same time Elvis Presley was stationed there), Derald has remained in our hometown. He worked for the city, at a Ford Motor dealership, and enjoyed an incredible 50-year career with the fire department, 35 years of it as the fire chief. During that time, he and Betty bought part of our childhood farm and built a house, raising kids, cattle, and growing hay and other crops.

None of us Delameters are very good at sitting still for too long, so after retiring and not knowing what to do with so much free time on his hands, Derald went back to work as a school bus driver for almost a decade. He still farms today, and he and Betty have created a sort of "hummingbird resort" they sit and watch from their big picture window. Whenever I'm in town I try to go by there to enjoy it with them.

My nickname for Twylia is "Sister T." While my other siblings were amusing, or serious, or strict, or quiet, Sister T has always been the naughty one!

When we were little and my parents would go to town on a Saturday night, they'd leave the younger three of us between her, Lillian, and Derald. I always looked forward to Sister T's "watch" because even though she did so with quiet Derald, if there was any mischief to be had, she was always ready and willing to be in the thick of it! When she was around, we got to try chewing tobacco, raid the refrigerator at-will, stay up late, and even let our hair down a bit with our language, all before our parents got home.

Sister T married Charles, a guy from Texas who originally came to Princeton with his company to install lines for the new dial phones. His job took them to several different states until they eventually moved to his hometown in Comanche, raising their three children plus the son of one of his relatives.

Decades later they divorced (she was the second in our immediate family to do so), which for us was taboo because we were raised that Delameters didn't get divorced. It was part family "rule" part social stigma that once married, you stayed married. You had made a commitment before God, your spouse, family, and friends, and that was that. If the marriage went sour, for whatever reason, you just had to find a way to stick it out.

Looking back I respect those in my family who felt they had to take this step, realizing that we don't have to do what we were taught, just because that was what we were taught. Life does what it does. And though very painful sometimes, for the best and highest good of all concerned, we just need to redirect our course.

Charles unfortunately was killed in a car accident, and Sister T moved to western Texas to be near their grown children. When their jobs started scattering them to the winds, she moved back to Princeton.

After being away for so many years, she's delighted to be back and to have a daily family connection. Now in her 80s and still very, very active, she's always got something going on. Her latest projects are gardening, reading, and learning how to quilt!

I was born six years after Sister T, the biggest gap in the sibling portion of our family tree. By then, most of them had moved away from home before I learned how to recite the alphabet. So, my upbringing was really with just my two younger siblings.

My brother Jerrie and I were both born in September, his arrival coming just five days before my first birthday. Although we celebrate "Labor Day" as a tribute to the contributions and achievements of the American workforce, I say mother is the one who named it!

When we were in middle school, Jerrie and I decided we were going to smoke. So we went to the local Ally-Martin drug store to buy cigarettes. When Jerrie asked how much they cost, the clerk said the unfiltered Camels were 23 cents a pack, and the Winstons were 27 cents a pack. Jerrie chose the Camels and I chose the Winstons, mainly because entertainer, comedian and game show host Gary Moore advertised them on television and in my mind, he was the ultimate man! Paying the extra money was totally worth it to be like him, and I remember leaving the store feeling very proud of the cigarettes now bouncing around in my t-shirt pocket!

Jerrie lived most of his life in Princeton, working as a mechanic and farmhand. He met and married a woman named Kay, they had one son, and bought the major portion of our family farm.

In the early '80s he was in a serious car accident that left him paralyzed from the waist down. But emotionally and physically he still did things most people wouldn't even consider doing from a wheelchair. Jerrie always had a real talent for building, so he was able to add ramps, additional rooms, and many other things to his home to get him where he needed to go and help him do what he needed to do. Not having the use of his legs was in no way going to stop him!

The baby of the family is my sister, Jo. She worked for a tractor air filter manufacturer for many years, married a man named Kenny, had two children, and then unfortunately divorced while they were still little. For me, going to visit her on Christmas and other times of the year is like going "home." She cooks like mother, acts like mother, and her house feels just like going back to Mom and Dad's.

As I write this book, H.A., George, Clay, Foster, Lillian, and Jerrie have already moved on to their next spiritual experiences.

George died in 1992, Clay in 1994, Foster in 2005, H.A. in 2010, Lillian in 2012, and Jerrie in 2016. All of their respective spouses, (except for Lenore, H.A.'s wife, and Kay, Jerrie's ex-wife) are deceased now as well.

They are all deeply missed.

As you might imagine, in a family of 13 overall there are lots of stories and lots of drama! Our family is so crazy that I say we are "One tent short of a full-blown circus!" But they are *MY* circus.

Over the years, despite each of us following our own religious, political, social, and other beliefs and ways of life—at times not always understanding what the others have said or done—we love each other dearly and have come to respect and accept each other for who we are.

We have an unbreakable bond that has stood the test of time and distance, and it remains strong to this day.

Chapter 4
<u>Grease in the Skillet</u>

Growing up I thought that my dad just didn't like me.

Up until I was born my parents had already raised five boys, and they each enjoyed doing all of the same farming duties just like my dad and how he was raised: milking cows, running tractors, going coon hunting, getting covered with hay seeds and sweat, and all those types of things - "manly stuff."

And I didn't want to do any of that.

Some of the things I really enjoyed, as far as manual labor was concerned, was mowing hay, cultivating the row crops, working in the garden, and growing flowers. I didn't know exactly why that was, but I could sit out there and do those things all by myself and just daydream.

I remember when I was in the 7th grade Jerrie and I sold packets of flower and veggie seeds for Earl May Garden Center. If we were able to sell 10 of them, we'd win a prize, or we could get new packets to keep for ourselves. Well, guess who would rather have the flower seeds over, say, the reward of a rod and reel? Nevertheless, since I also enjoyed fishing, Jerrie and I did choose a rod and reel prize another time!

At one point with all of my new seed packets, I was planting Zinnias next to the fence in front of our house, going to great lengths to make the rows just perfect. When they came up, hundreds of them, in fact, I was so excited and loved all over those flowers! They were red, orange, pink, yellow, purple, and some were multi-colored. And everyone who came to the house admired them, including my 3-year old niece who always insisted on bringing her momma a "pity" flower she picked.

As proud as I was of my colorful handiwork and the admiration that came with it, it kind of irked me when someone would take some without asking. As many of them as I had, you'd think it wouldn't have been that big of a deal. But I guess they were my babies and I was the protective parent.

I also remember, like it was yesterday, my mother telling me that the next time she went into Trenton (where she did her shopping) she would bring me a new rake and a hoe. This was a new luxury for our household to replace the ones we were using with broken or missing handles, or that were made "good as new" by my dad in his shop.

The day I knew she was going to the store I was so excited about it I could hardly contain myself! As soon as the school bus dropped me off at home and I'd changed into my home clothes, I ran back out onto the porch where my new tools were waiting for me. It was like Christmas morning! You would've thought she had given me something grand like a new bicycle, which would excite most kids.

Once out in the yard I began to rake and rake, getting everything all piled up to burn later that day. I was at the height of my glory. To this day, whenever I smell burning leaves my mind drifts back to that magnificent day.

It was also about that time that my Aunt Rose from Oregon was visiting. When she saw what "Little Johnnie" (there's a whole bunch of drama later in this book about why my name is spelled that way!) had done, she gave me 50 cents for my labor! A day or two later, after she had gone back home, I was still out there in my own personal heaven when mother reminded me that Aunt Rose wasn't there any longer to pay me.

"I'm not doing it for the money," I said, "I just like doing it!"

About 1955 or so, my family purchased another farm property next to where we lived. There was nothing on it but brush, rocks (rattlesnakes too!), and a large lilac bush from which I immediately dug up a few stems, replanting them in our yard. One of those relocated bushes has survived to this day, and the last time I was in Princeton I got to tell the current landowner where they came from.

As part our regular chores, Jerrie and I were supposed to help take care of the garden where our family had planted sweet corn, radishes, carrots, cabbage, turnips, beets, cucumbers, and lots of other vegetables. When it was time to do the work, he and I would go out there together, but within a few minutes he'd drift away into the shop to do something else, leaving me to take care of the planting, weeding, and overall care all by myself.

One year when the green beans were ready, and Jerrie of course had miraculously found something else to do, I picked the entire harvest and brought them into the house. Mother was ill that year, and when the ladies in the community found that out they came right over to spend the day canning. And they were just gushing about how "Jerrie and Johnnie" had stepped up to the plate, done all this work, and made sure the harvest wouldn't go to waste. Their praise even somehow made it into the community newspaper. *But I was the one who had done all of the work!* Jerrie hadn't done a thing, but he got half the credit! I was very upset about that at the time, but now my family and I get a good laugh when we think about his crafty ways of getting out of doing garden work.

As much as I loved my new garden tools, using tools in general just didn't float my boat. There were times when dad and I would be out in the shop or somewhere doing that "manly stuff" and I'd silently slip away and go back into the house. Next thing I know here he comes, dragging me back out there crying and carrying on. I didn't know why I didn't like to be out there … I just didn't. Yet I still felt a lot of guilt and shame for what I considered "not measuring up" by doing what he wanted me to do.

My passion and talents for making things look beautiful extended inside our home as well.

After Grandma Kelly (my mother's mother) passed, she left some money, and mother wanted to use part of it to buy some new furniture. So she and I went to Chuck George Furniture Store in town in search of a chrome dinette set with six chairs.

While we were there, she spotted an antique china cupboard that only cost $15. Even then, as a young elementary school kid, I was looking at those pieces—one very modern and the other very old—thinking, "Oh mother! These don't belong together in the same house!"

Our big Sunday meals when the whole family would get together was another place I was totally in my element. This was when all of the women were in the kitchen having a great time, and I was right in the middle of them listening to the talking, giggling, sad and funny stories, and watching how they prepared the food. But after a while they were like, "Now Johnnie, get out there with the men! You belong where the men are!"

I would grudgingly trudge out to the living room and listen to the men folk cussing and talking about mechanical repairs and stuff. But I didn't want to hear about how much grease you put in a crank case. I was more drawn to the female energy in the house and wanted to talk about the roast in the oven, how pretty mom's curtains went with her wallpaper, and grease in the skillet!

When I couldn't stand it any longer, I'd sneak back into the kitchen until one of my older sisters or my mother noticed I was back and say, yet again, "Now go back in the living room with the men where you belong!"

I soon learned (I think from a dog) that if I stood in the doorway between them, I could tune out what my dad and the other men were talking about in the living room, but still listen

31

to what the women were doing in the kitchen. I don't know if anyone ever noticed that, but either way, in that spot, everyone would pretty much leave me alone.

Five rambunctious, know-how-to-build-and-fix anything sons, then I come along and all I want to do is stay in the house, bake cookies, and grow flowers!

I'd heard my dad say, "John is just not like the other boys." But I don't know that my family knew what that was really about. It wasn't until I was in my 70s that a minister explained to me that it wasn't that my dad didn't like me for not being like the boys. It was that he didn't know what to do with me (this was waaaaay before the television show *Will and Grace* when being whatever shade of gay was OK!*). My parents had treated me the best way they could with what they knew, but they just didn't have a lot of information about being gay, something I didn't know I was yet, either.

I've often wondered if they ever sought help from anybody about my behavior. But knowing my dad, I doubt that he'd have ever brought it up. And my mother, probably out of shame, would've taken the position of, "What will people think of me if I have a gay son?"

I was once asked if there *was* a question in her mind if she'd have at least brought it up to my dad. But I doubt it because she was very secretive about things. I mean nowadays when in a group with friends, people will just say, for example, that they need to go to the bathroom. In my mother's day, you would *never* say that in front of a man! If she were here and she needed to go she would say something like, "I need to go to the back for just a little bit" - that type of thing. Women just didn't discuss "sensitive things" with other people, and especially not in front of a man. So no, "Different Johnnie" would probably not have been a topic of conversation.

But it *was* a topic of conversation in my head:

"I'm different."

"I somehow don't belong."

"Why can't I be like my brothers?"

"What if my parents reject me?"

"Something is really wrong with me."

I just wanted to be myself—whoever that was—and for everyone else to be OK with that.

Chapter 5
<u>Hell is a Gazillion degrees ... in the Shade</u>

In both the spring and fall, two-week-long revival services were a big part of my Baptist upbringing. It was a time when they pulled out all the stops to get you to join the church and be "saved."

There were visiting evangelists, guest musical soloists, fiery preaching and banging on the "sacred desk" (the pulpit, for you non-Baptists), altar calls, you name it. And just like Christmas, after all the hullabaloo, things went back to business as usual.

One of the evangelists who came to our church said he'd figured out the degree of hell - the temperature of it. And it was hot! That, of course, scared the, pardon the pun, "hell" out of me, and I thought I was going to burn down there forever!

At that particular time I was just entering puberty, that awkward stage when your body is really changing, your hormones are racing, and you're trying to figure out what's going on "down there." So naturally there was some physical exploration of the changes and feelings in my boy parts.

Now you have to remember that this was in the 1950s, and anything considered sexual in nature—either in the home or on television—wasn't discussed. And if the subject should come up it was generally naughty – especially in a religious setting.

So when I heard that evangelist say that one day we'd stand before God and all of our thoughts and deeds would be known to everyone, that was very frightening, and I just knew I was doomed.

His words got me thinking that Brother Harry, and my mother, and a whole bunch of other people (maybe even Santa Claus too!) would know what I'd been doing! I was unclean, a sinner, and touching myself was definitely a sin. I'd be traveling so fast to a hell so hot, there was nothing that was going to save me.

Now I don't want to slam the church, but some things there just aren't right - making us think that one wrong move and the land of fire and brimstone would be our eternal home. And the real shame behind that kind of thinking and religious philosophy is that it's based on fear. And it was sort of implied that any kind of relationship other than one between a man and a woman was wrong.

So naturally my mind went right to, "I'll NEVER do that again!" just in case there was any hope of sparing my body and soul from that red-hot and tragic end.

Like I said before, my dad never went to church, and my mother only went with us every once in a blue moon. She'd say it was because she was sick or had to stay home to fix meals for everybody, or some other reason.

So as you can imagine, many years later about a month before my father died, my early Baptist teachings about hell surfaced again, catching me totally off guard. Here he was, so close to death, with the added pain of not being a Christian. And because of this I thought he was going to die and burn in hell forever and we'd never see him again. What kind of God would do that to us?

Perhaps we all reexamine our connection to the God of our understanding when near our final moments on earth, because one night while my dad was in the hospital he said he started seeing angels and decided he really wanted to go to heaven. So, he said to God, "I'm ready if you'll have me," and just like that he personally accepted the Lord as his Savior.

Not too long after that my brother, George, and the minister from his church came to visit my dad. As they were talking, they asked if he'd be willing to share some of his life stories. It was then that they heard the full details of one we'd heard in bits and pieces over the years: When he was a teenager his mother—my grandmother—ran off with another man.

It happened at church.

My grandfather and grandmother and all of their children had gone to Sunday service, and at a pre-arranged time "the other man" came to get Grandma. My grandfather tried to stop them, but the guy beat him up, leaving him crying and despondent on the church steps.

My dad, who was a teenager at the time, was devastated, of course. Here was his big strong dad who could do anything, now emotionally and physically bruised and lying on the steps of God's house. To make matters worse, all of this happened just as the congregation, which included all of his friends, was getting out to go home for lunch.

The only part of the story that we in the family knew, which is what my mother had told us, was that daddy's mother "had run away with Old Bob." We didn't know any of the other details.

The really sad part of it is that for most of his life he had no one to talk to about this horrific event in his life. And I'm pretty sure Mother didn't know the whole story either. I'm guessing that the trauma and humiliation of that experience is why he never went to church.

It was the only testimony he gave before he died.

When he took his last breath, I remember thinking, "Well, bye now," and there was so much peace that came over me.

Hell may have been a gazillion degrees in the shade, but at least my daddy wasn't going to burn down there for all of eternity.

Chapter 6
New Branches on the Family Tree

There were a few "always" scenarios about me growing up:

I was always being called a momma's boy.

I was always being called a sissy.

And I always had a girlfriend.

In grade school I thought having a girlfriend meant having a friend who was a girl. So of course, I had plenty of them!

And if I had a girlfriend, that meant I wasn't a sissy.

All of that changed in high school when I met Eva Streett.

Living in a small town where news travels fast, I'd heard that a new family with six kids had settled into the Princeton area the previous winter. The first time I saw Eva (pronounced eh-vah) was at a farm auction where a group of girls was selling sandwiches for the 4H Club.

Among them were two I didn't know who turned out to be the two "Streett girls" all the guys had been going gaga over since they moved into town. Even though enrolled in a different high school than me and my friends, they had already created quite a buzz!

My first real opportunity to talk to Eva was during one of our cruising nights down at the local Tastee Freez.

My buddies and I were making the rounds in my brother Jerrie's pride and joy—a black 1941 Ford Coupe. I, on the other hand, had my eyes on that beautiful 1959 Ford Galaxy. On the TV show "Perry Mason," Raymond Burr had a convertible version of that same car. And even though we had a black and white TV, I just knew his was black with a red interior as well!

"Perry" was the ultimate man: polished, professional, he wore great suits to dinner, and he got to cruise around with his beautiful secretary "Della Street" (it's kind of a funny coincidence that Della and Eva, although spelled differently, had the same last name!).

So, our summer days and nights were filled with groups of guys cruising around in their cool shiny cars, shouting cat calls at the girls. Each time we made another pass by The Haven truck stop, around the square, through the park past the swimming pool, and back around to the Tastee Freez, I'd try to get Eva's attention by yelling another, what I thought was a "must know" fact about my dream car.

I had a more civilized opportunity to get to know her a little better when she and some other people from her church visited ours for the twice-a-year revivals.

Our first date was in the spring of 1961.

Our church youth group was traveling to Edinburg, about 40 minutes south of Princeton, where I was going to be one of the featured speakers. Because my dad wouldn't let me drive that far yet, I had to ride with some of the other members. A few nights before our presentation, I found out there would only be three of us in the carpool and the other two were "going steady." I definitely didn't want to be the third wheel, so I called Eva to see if she wanted to go with me, and she accepted my invitation.

On the way home that night I remember thinking she seemed like a real special girl. She was tall, thin, a brunette, an extrovert, very down-to-earth, and she liked music. We also had a lot in common: she was raised on a farm, and was a church girl, which was very important. Later on I learned she had glasses that didn't get tangled up with mine when we kissed! It wasn't long before we were going steady too, and I jokingly told people I had my first "street girl!"

Since we lived in opposite directions from the center of town, it was a bit of a haul to go back and forth to see her. One time my dad said to me, "You're not going to make a habit of this, are you? Because it sure takes a lot of gas to date her!"

But I was bull-headed. My attitude was, "That's what you think!"

Two months later, in May, Eva, who like all of my earlier "girlfriends" was a year older than me, graduated and immediately moved to Kansas City where she'd gotten a job as a long line operator with AT&T (if you remember the classic scenes with comedienne Lilly Tomlin's character "Ernestine" on the TV show *Laugh-In* you'll get the general picture!). In June, at the ripe old age of 16, I asked her to marry me. And she said yes.

We decided to keep our engagement a secret until Christmas. By then I'd be "older" at 17, a few months from graduation, and able to buy her an engagement ring (after the sale of a few sheep, I had the money!).

Near the end of my senior year I started looking for a job in Kansas City to be near Eva. A friend told me they were hiring people at a Sears Roebuck & Co. warehouse to do simple manual line labor duties, so I figured that my dyslexia, poor penmanship, and not-so-good grades wouldn't be a problem. But when I found out the company would only be keeping people for about three months, so they didn't have to pay unemployment benefits, I had to come up with a different plan.

Maybe that was for the best, because when I got there I wouldn't have had a place to live, I didn't have a car, and although there was public transportation, learning how to navigate all of that seemed so overwhelming for this small town farm kid.

It was then that I decided it might be a good idea to move to Lincoln where my sister Lillian was living. She had a good job working for the *Back to the Bible* radio broadcast, it was walking distance from where she lived, and everything you would need like groceries, clothes, and all of that was close by.

I talked to Eva about it and although she too was disappointed I wouldn't be near her in Kansas City, she thought it was a good idea.

In Lincoln, Lillian was good enough to let me live with her while I looked for a job and earned enough money to settle into my own place. And bless her heart, she even loaned me her car for the first year so I could get around. I think she was really happy to have me there, and to be able to keep an eye out to make sure her little brother didn't get into any trouble!

I was hoping to get a job at *Back to the Bible* as well, but that fell through. However, I did find one at The Journal Star Printing Company where I was hired on as a dispatcher.

I really liked the work and saved as much money as I could to be able to go back and forth to spend time with my future bride in Princeton whenever we both went there to visit our families.

* * *

Eva and I got married in a lovely ceremony, followed by a wonderful reception, on September 1, 1962. After the honeymoon she moved to live with me in Lincoln, and the following week she got a job in the accounting department at a Miller & Payne department store.

Looking back, I see that although I didn't consciously plan it this way, my marriage was very different from that of my parents.

They stuck to very traditional roles, in that the men were the ones who worked and provided for the family, while the women stayed home and took care of the cooking, the cleaning, and the kids. Mother and my sisters could occasionally work in the garden and the yard, but NEVER in the fields. That was just my dad's belief.

I remember that we had a neighbor one time where we saw the ladies go out and milk the cows, drive the tractors, and things like that. But daddy didn't approve of that at all. I think he believed women had rights, yet still he kind of made all the decisions. For example, there would be times when I'd ask my mother about something and she'd say, "Well, I have to talk to Daddy about that." That was what it was like back then, but I still think they were very happy together with the life and family they had built.

Speaking of starting a family, my dad never talked to me much about girls, or relationships, or how to create a strong marriage. And certainly nothing about sex. What little I knew I'd heard from my friends in the neighborhood and the guys at school, who of course all had great stories about what they supposedly did.

Eva and I were both virgins, and our first sexual experience of was on our wedding night. Based on the male versions of the stories I'd heard, I had great expectations of the wedding night being the most important in our entire relationship and the best sex we ever had. And from what I understand, Eva's friends and the girls at work had been talking her up with a bunch of female fantasies like "not seeing the light of day" for days on end. Or that she'd be cooking, and I'd come home, silently turn off the skillet and … The descriptions were everything found in a Harlequin romance book and more!

After all that time we'd waited, and the anticipation that went hand-in-hand with it, our first time wasn't as rewarding as I thought it would be. And I could see that Eva seemed let down too. She probably hadn't learned anything about relationships or marriage when growing up either. Sadly, both of us only knew what we'd heard from our friends and what little we saw on TV.

We never talked about our relationship much and just soldiered on, with the ultimate "goal" of having children. And we finally did.

Beth was born in 1965. Five years later, due to some physical issues Eva had been experiencing (which resulted in a hysterectomy) we adopted a son, David. She and I always say that one of our children came *out of* our hearts, and the other came *into* our hearts.

We were a complete family, enjoyed living in Lincoln, and life was good.

We attended a lovely church we liked very much called Southview Baptist where we settled in nicely and went to services regularly. Although it had some of the same teachings of my youth, including that hell was just one misstep away from us all, I felt comfortable enough to stay.

44

At Southview Baptist I say we were a church outside of a church. We got out of the pews and did what we said we as a spiritual community were going to do. If someone needed help finishing their basement, or if there was a family in need of food, or anything else that arose, it was nothing for several of us to just show up and help. That's just the way we were.

As we became more active there, we both sang in the choir, and Eva became a nursery coordinator and worker, which was a joyous responsibility for her because she had always loved babies! I began volunteering to drive the church bus, serve on several committees, and eventually became a deacon and well-respected in our community.

Our home life was busy as well, a lot of it doing things with and for Beth and David. And I didn't fully appreciate until we had kids how much time and energy it takes just to keep up! Although we were only in our 20s, working, raising children, and having a church and social life were sometimes exhausting. In comparison, by the time my parents started raising me, Jerrie, and Jo, they were in their late 50s or early 60s and had had a lot of practice. But the one drawback was come 5 o'clock at night they were tired, and we were active teenagers still wanting to roll. At the time, I just didn't understand why they didn't want to roll with us as well, and I don't know that they could fully understand why we wanted to keep going either. All we heard at the end of the day was, "It's time to be quiet."

Eva and I were still only in our 30s when my parents passed. And as my children continued growing up, I felt really cheated that they weren't around to see how much they changed, and what they were doing, and what kind of father and husband I had become.

I had friends whose parents were coming to their grandchildren's school concerts, and birthday parties, and over for the holidays, and all of that. But I had no parents around who could do those things too. Their absence left a big empty hole in my heart.

It wasn't until my friends' parents' health started to decline, and they had to put them into rest homes, or were sitting around crying, trying to decide what to do because their mom or dad's mind was gone, that I realized what a blessing it was that my parents passed very quickly.

My dad, who had been suffering from cancer, was still very active. He farmed in the spring and passed peacefully, at age 72, over Labor Day weekend. Seven months later my mother, who seemed to be adjusting to her new normal pretty well, had a heart attack and died. She was only 67 years old.

Although glad they went so fast and didn't linger for months or years like some other people's parents, it was still a great loss. Not just for me, but because my kids and the rest of their grandchildren missed out on seeing *their* life.

Beth and one of her cousins, Paul, who recently passed away, have always cherished their memories of sitting on grandad's lap while he held his coffee cup and added a big ole heaping scoop of sugar, just letting the coffee kind of drift over it.

When he finished drinking it, he'd let the kids stick their little fingers in there to get all the sugar left out of the bottom of the cup. It's a sweet memory she'll always have, in more ways than one.

Eva's parents lived well into their 70s and 80s and were as active as they could be in Beth and David's lives. They got to ride in their Grandad's car, and visit with cousins, aunts, and uncles. Her parents attended special school and church events, cooked big family meals for everyone, made sure that for Christmas there were lots of presents and cookies under the tree, and whenever they sent cards or letters to the house, they always included two sticks of gum for each of the kids (they still remember that, even to this day).

I'm very thankful for the time and love Eva's parents put into our family. Yet it's still sad knowing that my kids didn't get to have my parents in their lives for very long.

But life still goes on and you keep trying to do the best you can.

Chapter 7
<u>Waiting in Line for the Restroom</u>

Growing up, I didn't know anything about being gay—I was just "different"—and I thought my attraction to boys was because I'd seen them undressed in the locker rooms during gym class and at the swimming pool.

I grew up with a lot of shame around those thoughts, with the added burden of society and religious influences that said being "different" was wrong.

I've learned that many men who think they may be homosexual do the best they can to stave off any "ill thoughts" until right around their mid-30s, eventually feeling like they just have to go ahead and try it. Then there's the idea that "As soon as I get married that'll all change and I'll want a woman."

Well, surprise, surprise! It doesn't, and it didn't.

In the early years of my marriage to Eva, those thoughts were swirling around in my head even stronger than before. I'd heard that sometimes straight men trying to "get off" have to think about some gorgeous babe. When having sex with Eva, I had to pretend I was in bed with another man just to fulfill myself. Rock Hudson, James Arness, and Michael Landon were some of the hotties that came to mind. But of course, all of this lustful thinking just added to my shame, and guilt, and feeling like I was less of a man. And I was going to hell because of it; separated from God forever in a burning hell!

What was wrong with me? I had married my high school sweetheart, and she was a truly good woman and a good wife. We had two beautiful children. We loved our home, community, church, and jobs. To the outside observer, we had "a perfect life."

Some men stay in their marriages, some turn to a homosexual lifestyle, and others straddle the fence forever. I didn't quite know what I was going to do, but as more and more time went on our home life continued to tumble downward.

***

Exploring my sexuality outside of our marriage began about 7 or 8 years after Eva and I said, "I do."

Frequently, when using the men's restroom in a department store, or restaurant, or somewhere else, I'd see handwritten messages in the stalls from guys looking for action. But I didn't think they were real. I mean, we're only in there for a few minutes anyway!

But I soon learned that if you're in there for a longer period of time, you'll sometimes see a steady flow of people going in...and staying. Since I didn't have anything else to go on as far as meeting men, I started hanging out longer as well.

That's when I got propositioned for the first time.

It was in the Lincoln train station. I was already in the restroom when this cute guy came in. We started checking each other out, made a few gestures back and forth, moved to where no one could see us, and two minutes later it was done (I was young then!).

So this is what I'd been missing all my life! I had finally connected with someone sexually who was of the same mindset. It was a very bittersweet moment, because although I'd found what my soul had been longing for, and it was so good and fulfilling, I was married, full of guilt and shame, and like I'd heard before, I would surely be going straight to hell.

It's interesting what our minds come up with when we're confused or struggling. Part of me rationalized that because I wasn't cheating on my wife with another woman, it wasn't as bad as it could have been. But it was still wrong, and "I will never do this again!" I thought.

But the next day, I was back in the restroom, and it wasn't long before I had multiple male sexual encounters on the side.

And it didn't help my sexual identity struggles that I had a lot of other turmoil going on in my life right about that time.

My parents had died.

It was the end of the Vietnam War and there was profound tension in the air because of the horrible mental, emotional, and physical state a lot of them were in when they came back home.

And Eva and I were experiencing financial troubles.

By about 1975, living this lie was really beginning to take its toll. The energy in our household was strained, and I was depressed about not living up to my responsibilities as a husband and father.

I suppose I could have asked for a divorce, but I really wanted to try and make it work, especially for the kids.

Many years later I had an opportunity to talk to Beth and David about that time in our lives. They said they were really glad I was there when they were young, and they've thanked me for staying. I think they understood that I was doing the best I could to be around for them, despite how miserable I was.

Even though I hadn't reconciled myself to it yet, I was very gay, very religious, and I just knew I could get this changed.

Chapter 8
<u>The Elephant in the Room</u>

The first time I ever tasted alcohol, I was about 9 or 10 years old.

I'd seen some of my older brothers have a beer now and again, and although it was rare for my dad to drink in front of us, I knew that he did pretty frequently. His side of the family, I learned years later, was heavy into the sauce as well.

Although I didn't know what "drunk" meant at the time, that's how he'd often come home.
Dad, my brother Jerrie, and I would be working in the fields, something would break, and Dad would have to go into town to buy a part to fix it. But he wouldn't come back.

As the day wore on, I noticed that my mother got more and more quiet. Not only did she not have much to say, but any questions we asked received short, one-to-three-word answers.

Then by early evening one of my brothers or a brother-in-law would be driving dad's car with him in it, with another brother in a car behind them. While helping Dad into the house I was told that "he didn't feel well," and I eventually figured out that this was what they called "drunk."

The next morning there was a lot of silence between him and my Mom, and within a few days everything slowly went back to normal. A week, or sometimes a month or two would go by, and this scene would play out again.

One day I found one of my Dad's bottles in the barn, and out of curiosity I decided to try it. After making sure no one was around, I carefully screwed off the top, took a little sip, and yuk! It was awful! Why in the world would anyone want to drink something like this, I thought.

Later I had "sippers remorse," my actions yet another reason why I was going to hell because "only sinners drink."

Now back on the straight and narrow, I never took another drink, even in high school when my peers and others around me were drinking. "I don't drink" is how I answered their inquiries, to which they often replied something like, "Oh yeah 'you religious people' don't drink!"

After moving to Lincoln, I was shocked to see some of my female co-workers drinking when we went out to lunch. In Princeton you rarely saw a woman take a drink, so I just assumed they did things differently "in the big city."

I'd order a sandwich and ice-tea or coffee, and the others would say, "You know, you can order a drink, John."

"I don't believe in drinking," I'd answer.

"Oh, you're religious!" was their reply.

Although this razzing was not as strong as in high school, it took me back to my internal messaging about not fitting in – that something was wrong with me and I wasn't good enough.

That all changed when I hit my mid-20s.

Every year on the day of the office Christmas party we'd go in, get any necessary work done by 9:30, take our mid-morning break, then go back to our work areas and start drinking whatever we'd brought for the festivities.

I always just drank coffee or a coke.

One day, I decided I wanted to fit in. It was time to show everyone that I DID belong.

One of the BYOB concoctions was this punch made with vodka and cranberry juice (among other things) and I loved it! Being an all-or-nothing kind of guy I had a glass, felt a little bit of a buzz, my inhibitions started falling away, and I had another. Now we were all laughing and joking, and I remember thinking, "Everyone likes me!"

The fact that I'd never done anything like this before (besides that first little sip in the barn) made me want to drink even more. I was now part of the "in crowd." Another glass of the good stuff followed, and it wasn't long before I was, as they say, three sheets to the wind.

Our little A.M. office happy hour was followed by the company holiday luncheon at the Nebraska Club downtown. It had always been a sort of formal affair with a wonderful elaborate meal, and here we 20-somethings show up drunk (the executives of the company were drinking too, but they were older and knew how to handle their liquor!).

By the time lunch and the rest of the afternoon party was over, I somehow managed to get sober enough to drive home. Like my Dad all those years ago, I told my family I wasn't feeling well and went straight to bed.

The next morning I told Eva that I'd had a drink at the party and the first question she asked was, "Well, what did it taste like?" I was expecting a little bit of anger and a reminder from her about how "we don't drink," so that relieved me of a lot of the guilt I'd been carrying around since the day before.

From then on it was a slow but steady snowballing drinking habit.

Those previous polite declines to invitations to stop at the bar across the street for a drink after work became yesses. "I'll just have one," became two, then three, then ... The only reason I started slowing down was because money was very tight. AND I had to drive home!

Every couple of months someone from work would throw a party at a bar, their home, or around a pond on some private acreage, and anywhere between 20 to 40 people would show up – all drinking and having a good time. I was invited to those get-togethers as well.

"I wasn't 'In' in high school, but I am now," was my thinking, and that slow but steady snowball soon became an avalanche.

The drinking, combined with the struggles over my sexuality, led to a lot of "drop out guy" stuff in many areas of my life, as well as a lot of frustration and anger from Eva.

"Drunk again!" she'd say when I stumbled in the front door, to which I'd reply with a smart ass, slurred answer like, "Yeah? Me too!"

It hurts me to admit that I didn't know what effect it had on her and the kids, because I was off in my own little world. I wonder now if any of that has continued on down the branches of the family tree.

Years later, in Alcoholics Anonymous (A.A.), I learned that Dad was what is called a "Periodic Alcoholic" or "Binge Drinker" – someone who when something goes wrong needs a drink to "fix it." And because they have some sort of control over it, they convince themselves that they don't have a drinking problem. But once that next drink hits their lips...

These addictive behaviors, whether it's to alcohol, drugs, sex, food, work, religion, or anything else, and the inability or unwillingness to talk about it, creates havoc in everyone's life.

My drinking was all about trying to fit in and trying to "fix" myself - my sexuality, my low self-esteem, and that overall feeling that something was wrong with me.

My dad would drink when something "broke."

Turns out I was the one who was broken.

Chapter 9
<u>Compassion Speaks to all Faiths</u>

For the most part, our life in Lincoln appeared to roll right along as "normal."

The kids, now ages 8 and 13, were doing well between their paper routes, playdates, and children's and youth choir activities. Beth was participating in Brownies and YMCA Indian Princesses, and David and I were busy with the YMCA Indian Guides for fathers and sons, and various sports. With all of that going on, life was busy but good.

Eva and I had also started a little business selling Plaster Craft. Real popular in the '70s and '80s, these were ceramic-like products you could paint; everything from statues, to busts, vases, decorative pedestals, figurines, holiday crafts, and so on. The main difference is that they didn't have to be fired in a kiln so anyone could simply paint and enjoy them. We bought a few pieces once while on vacation and liked painting them so much we started buying more. Before you knew it, we had started a little "store" in our basement, selling them to our neighbors and friends for a couple of years.

We eventually opened a real storefront, "The House of Plaster," which Eva ran full-time, and when I wasn't at work, I did all the handyman type things around the shop. Although not a real money maker for us, we managed to keep the store going for six years. When the price of gas suddenly jumped up to a whopping 89.9 cents a gallon and people stopped buying crafts in order to be able to pay for gas and food, we were forced to sell the business.

Over the years our home had always been kind of an informal daycare, which Eva loved and was very good at doing. So, once our store closed and the word got out that Eva was available again, she got a whole new crop of kids to take care of.

I, on the other hand, decided to apply again to the *Back to the Bible* broadcast and was hired to work in their printing department.

Unfortunately, faced with the pressures of trying to be a good husband and family man while also running around having sex with men whenever I could, my drinking continued. As a result, I started having major back and ulcer problems. So I went to a doctor who was big on prescribing valium, and low and behold—those problems went away!

But now, even though I eased up on the booze a little bit, the valium soon became my new escape. And I was escaping often. So much so that every once-in-a-while Eva would tell me, "The pills you're taking for your back are making you a bit loopy."

To my knowledge she had no idea I was doubling or tripling up on my meds.

Despite all of this, while in Lincoln there were several events that became significant turning points in my life.

Two gentlemen who had come to town to establish a Baptist Student Union on the campus of the University of Nebraska, were invited by my church to come and speak.

What really struck me was how differently they talked about God. It was like they had a personal relationship with Him; like they were best friends. There was no fear, or strict adherence to "His rules," or anything like that. It just seemed like they had this peaceful connection with a friend they could call on the phone.

At that time, the church leadership was also engaged in a new minister search and they had invited Pastor Dennis Wood from Mobile, AL to give a trial sermon. Pastor Dennis was very clear about what he believed would be the right way to lead and grow our church, but not just in terms of increasing the number of congregants. He had a vision for how to lead and grow us *spiritually.*

In addition, his trial sermon lacked any kind of reference to the image of God that I had, which was a man with a long beard sitting on a throne wearing a white cloak who was out to get me! Like the men from the Baptist Student Union, he spoke of a warm, caring God; one who was here to love and support us as we traveled along life's path. A God that could see our perfection in everything and would walk beside us every step of the way.

That kind of teaching was exactly what my spirit was looking for, and I wanted what they seemed to have. That's when the substance abuse started falling away and I started attending church—which had dropped off somewhat—more regularly with my family.

I loved what I was hearing and felt like I was making great progress, and things got a lot better for a few weeks. Yet no matter how hard I tried, I just couldn't control my sexual urges and fell into rolling highs and lows of success then failure about stopping on my way home from Bible study to have sex with some guy.

This lack of self-control was so frustrating, to say the least, and I had no idea what to do about it.

And then, one Sunday evening during the service there was a slideshow presentation called, "Listen to the Butterflies." There were about 8 to 10 projectors placed around the room casting images that faded in and out onto the main screen in front. There we watched the life cycle of a butterfly as it goes through a complete metamorphosis from an egg, to a larva (caterpillar), pupa (wrapped in a silk cocoon), and finally into a colorful and fully formed butterfly. The woman presenting the slideshow said that each of these four transformation stages serve a specific purpose.

The part that really got my attention was the pupa. Sometimes looking very ugly and shriveled up like it's dying, it hangs from a tree branch, literally, by a thread, for a few weeks or longer before dropping to the ground below.

In that moment I thought, "If I don't get help with these struggles with my sexuality, I'm either going to hang on this painful branch forever, or eventually dry up, let go, fall off, and die."

The time had come to start my own metamorphosis. I knew I just couldn't go on hanging on by a thread any longer. I wanted and needed to be set free.

Although I felt comfortable with the leadership at Southview Baptist, I certainly had a lot of fear around going to them for help with "my problem." The only person I knew I could talk to was Pastor Dennis. It was a risk, and I had no way of knowing what might happen. But I was pretty sure he loved me and would help me.

Before the evening was over, I went to him and said, "I have to talk to you. And don't let me talk myself out of talking to you. I really need your help." So we set up an appointment for the following day.

For what felt like hours I sat in his office, spilling my guts about my thoughts, behaviors, and the fact that no one in my family knew. It was the first time I had actually expressed any of this outside of my own head, and it took everything I had to say the words. The internal turmoil and depression had been completely overwhelming for years, and I just couldn't hold onto it any longer.

Pastor Dennis just sat there, looked at me with tears welling up in his eyes, and gently said, "As far as I know, I don't know another gay person. But I want you to know that I love you, and I respect you, and I'm going to do whatever I can to help you and your family through this."

We prayed, his voice cracking a little bit as he spoke, and I could tell he did indeed love me and really cared about me and my family.

Looking back, this may have been a situation of "the blind leading the blind," since he didn't know much about the gay community. And I was so emotionally wrapped up in my life falling apart, I was in a total fog about what to think, say, or do. After a few months of counseling, Pastor Dennis referred me to a great therapist, all three of us believing I could be "fixed." I was completely set in the mindset that if we could find out what caused "this," then we could fix it. That's just the way it was back then.

As relieved as I felt to have found a safe place where I could share my story and fears, the therapy was going to cost $25 an hour (If I'd known how much it would cost in present day money, and how many years I'd spend in therapy, I would've stocked up on prepayments!). With a wife and two kids our budget was already strained. And of course Eva didn't know anything about my issues, much less about the therapy. So I had to get crafty about pulling that $25 a session out of there. I felt bad about going behind her back, but at this point I didn't know what else to do.

The therapy continued about once a month for quite a bit of time. When I could no longer afford it, Pastor Dennis referred me to someone else who thankfully helped me free of charge.

By this time, I'd started sharing my "dilemma" with a few male friends that I trusted. I had come to recognize then, and still tell people now, that Southview Baptist was a very unique church in many ways. For one, despite the culture around homosexuality in the mid-70's, there were people accepting of those of us struggling with our sexual identity. And they were more than willing to do all they could to help.

Secondly, that caring group was wise beyond their years— most of them, including Pastor Dennis, only in their late 20's. At age 32 I felt like the elder statesmen among them, and as far as I knew no one else in the group had ever known another gay man besides me.

While undergoing therapy and opening myself up more and more to those trusted friends, I refrained from having sex with anyone other than Eva. Despite my best intentions to "do right by her," it was a strain since we both knew (although not for the same reason) that although there physically, I was emotionally absent.

Making matters worse was watching couples around us enjoying what we didn't: public displays of affection, intimate whispers, and a general ease and obvious love for each other. Eva and I were just existing, dragging along from day-to-day. I'm sure the kids instinctively picked up on that lack of connection between us, but we sadly just didn't have it to give.

64

Eva eventually sought counseling and support from Pastor Dennis as well. She had no idea how to deal with my distant behavior or very unpredictable mood swings, like shutting down if someone looked at me in what I thought was a weird way. Or sitting in my living room chair like a zombie for hours, sometimes for an entire weekend.

The inability to connect with Eva emotionally also had another layer to it. Like most of us, she had had some childhood issues in her life. But our communication was so poor at that point, and she was trying so hard to figure out what was going on with me, that she probably didn't have the energy or the wherewithal to address them.

With all of this going on, there eventually came a point when I started feeling so shameful about my desires for men, guilt over what the kids might be feeling, my disconnect with Eva, and most of all, not being able to find a solution, that I just couldn't handle it any longer. I had tried really hard for an entire year to suppress these feelings, but it just wasn't working.

So, I went "back out," as they call it.

And like so many times before, after returning home feeling like the worst husband and father on earth, I'd say to myself, "I'm never going to do this again." That proclamation would last four or five days, then I'd get all excited about finding new and even more creative sexual experiences, only to return home to repeat the same excruciating self-loathing cycle.

When the self-disgust got high enough, I would confess (again) to the group at church. Even though I kept committing adultery (although it was with men, not women) and the effect my distance and behavior were most certainly having on Eva and the kids, those wonderful brothers still held my hand.

They never failed to offer a lot of love, acceptance, and compassion for my attempts at trying to do the right thing, while still working toward figuring out what was wrong with me.

I can't begin to express enough how unique, loving, and supportive Southview Baptist and those men were. Not just to me, but for others in the church with different mental, emotional, and spiritual needs.

Decades later I visited Pastor Dennis and his wife, Sandy, after they had moved to Arizona, and we shared so many fond memories of our time in Lincoln.

"I don't know about you," he said, "but we've pastored several churches around the country and have been unable to find, or create what we had in Lincoln."

"You're right," I agreed. "We've moved around the country as well and could never find the same sense of community we found there."

It wasn't long before my Lincoln "support team" thought it was time to tell Eva what was going on and make her a part of my healing process. Maybe she could help me make it through this.

"It's not really fair for her not to know what's going on," Pastor Dennis said.

He was right, of course. Keeping her in the dark was very unfair and agonizing for us both.

"But I don't even know where to *start* to tell her," I replied anxiously.

"Just hold her," he said. "Walk into the kitchen, and hold her, and say that you have to tell her something."

Bless Eva's heart, the night I came clean the first things she said were, "What did I do to cause this?" and "How can I fix it?"

She was thinking it was her fault.

I tried my best to explain that it wasn't her fault; that I'd had these feelings for years. They went as far back as my early church days when I was still so little my feet couldn't reach the floor; when I'd turn my body around in the pew to look back at the high school boys behind me. I didn't have a name for it then, and oddly enough I still couldn't bring myself to say the word I now knew—"gay."

All I could manage to utter was, "I don't know what you can do. The people I'm working with don't know either. But we're working toward getting this changed."

Eva, now with this new information, continued going for counseling at the church - at first just with Pastor Dennis, then the three of us together, and later alone with his wife, Sandy. After a while we all agreed that having Eva share her struggles with some of the wives of the guys I'd been talking to might help her understand a few more things as well.

"What's wrong with me?" and "How did I not see this?" was and still are very common questions when the woman in your life experiences the smashing of her fairytale. Most every little girl and young woman's dream is of finding a loving and doting soul mate, planning the wedding, choosing the bridesmaids and flowers and colors, having children, and living happily ever after ... all of it gone the moment they realize the guy they married is gay.

Eva and I tried our best to keep going, not quite living as roommates or in separate beds like Lucy and Desi and the other 1950s-era couples we grew up watching on television, but as normal as possible, mainly for Beth and David's sake.

Despite this, I kept looking for sexual satisfaction from men in bars and other gay hangouts. My addiction was so strong, and I had absolutely no willpower to fight it for more than a few days at a time.

Although Eva never confronted me, she knew what I was doing. She'd figure things out and say something like, "It sure took you a long time at the grocery store," or ask, "Was traffic heavy?" when I arrived home later than expected.

I wish I'd had the strength to say, "Well, I was out looking for something. I'm not happy in this."

In retrospect, we were both so unhappy and so closed off to our feelings and each other, I guess we figured if neither of us spoke about it, then we wouldn't have to face the facts and feel the pain of knowing what was happening between us was real and that I was gay, and we probably weren't going to make it. And I was single-handedly destroying our family.

We danced around it, but we just couldn't say anything. We just couldn't.

It's true when they say trying to get rid of fear is often scarier than living with it. We stay in that fearful place because in a weird way it's the easy thing to do. It's familiar. We know what to expect. I think of it as smoking another cigarette when you know how bad it is for your health. Or going back to the frig for another carton of ice cream even though you "are determined" to lose all of that unhealthy weight. Or staying in a physically or emotionally abusive relationship even when you know you deserve better.

I'm not sure if the guilt-and-shame cycle I kept deteriorating into was worse before Eva knew, or now that she did. My only thought was working as hard as I could to find out how to "fix me." And once I'd discovered that, then I could stop. I could be straight. We could live a normal life. I could give Eva her happily ever-after.

Little did I know that I'd spend *years* trying to figure out what "caused me" to be gay.

Chapter 10
<u>The City of Gold</u>

In 1982, after 20 years in Lincoln, we moved to the little town of Dahlonega, GA located about 65 miles north of Atlanta.

Its nickname is "The City of Gold" and there's a lot of interesting history behind that, including the Dahlonega Gold Museum State Historic Site and the annual Dahlonega Gold Rush Days Festival.

Whatever the history, I felt like moving here was the "golden ticket" out of my double life in Lincoln.

Before the move I'd gotten a job here at a company called Christian Financial Concepts, and Eva was hired to work in the main office. We all settled in just fine, renting this beautiful old home called The Rock House, a Dahlonega landmark built during the Depression out of quartz rock mined from the surrounding land. And we were grateful to have found another Baptist church here with a lot of loving, caring people. But it was nothing like what we had in Lincoln, so being without a support group or getting any kind of counseling certainly didn't help our marriage.

Dahlonega was another new town and another chance to make a clean break. I was no longer drinking or misusing prescription drugs, and as far as sex with men I said to myself (for the hundredth time), "I won't do it again! It's a small town and if I get caught it'll be bad."

I now had a safety net: the watchful eyes of a one-horse town that would surely keep me on the straight (no pun intended) and narrow, or so I thought.

In general, everyday life here with Eva and the kids was everything you might anticipate, except that the only "gold rush" going on was my haste to come up with any excuse to leave town in search of male companionship in nearby Gainesville or Atlanta.

The cycle was continuing, and I felt so powerless, alone, and still without any answers on how to stop it.

One night, Eva and I were unpacking some boxes. When I started taking them up to the attic she said, "We might as well get rid of those."

"But we'll need them when we move," I answered.

"Well, if we do, it'll be just a local move and we won't need all of them at one time."
Without thinking I said, "I don't think so. I just don't think we're going to stay here very long."

I can only imagine what she must have been thinking. We were only about two months into a move clear across the country from where we'd uprooted the kids and left our families and friends, and now I'm saying we need to hold onto these boxes because we might need to do it all over again!

I didn't know how else to explain it to her.

I just knew I wouldn't be able to stay here.

Chapter 11
Kansas City, Here We Come!

Two years later we packed up those boxes in the attic I'd insisted on keeping and moved from Dahlonega to Kansas City. It was another new phase for our family; another good clean break from the secret, double life I was living.

Driving west along Interstate 70 I yet again told myself, "I'm done with this, and I'm NEVER going to do it again."

For some reason I didn't realize how many times I'd said that before.

We weren't sure if we'd really like living in Kansas City. For small town people it was certainly much bigger than Princeton, and Dahlonega, and even Lincoln. But we wanted to continue working for a Christian organization and there were several throughout the area. And we'd also be close to family.

I'd gotten a position as a printer for the Nazarene Publishing House which started about eight days after we got into town, and we were fortunate that Eva was again hired on as well. Although I didn't agree with all of their theology, the company was very loving, caring, and good to their people, and we both loved working there.

By this time Beth had just graduated from high school back in Dahlonega, and David would be starting his freshman year of high school here.

To get the lay of the land and take some time to figure out where we really wanted to live, we rented a house for about a year. Then we bought a pretty little fixer-upper just north of downtown in the community of Gladstone, which felt like a small town although very close to the "big city."

We also joined a local church, simply because it was close by, there was no traffic to deal with to get there, and parking was a breeze! It was a very good church with very good people, but spiritually I wasn't getting what I needed.

However, there was another one I'd heard about from the youth minister we had in Dahlonega. He'd gone to seminary in the Kansas City area and always spoke very fondly of a place called Broadway Baptist Church. It was a bit of a drive from Gladstone to Midtown where the church was located, but he'd had so many great things to say about it, I really wanted to give it a try.

The first time I ventured in that direction I just wanted to drive by and see what it looked like. But something about it spoke to me immediately, so I went home and told Eva I wanted to attend a service there.

"I'm teaching Sunday School and working in the nursery," she said of her new duties at the church near our house.

"Well, we've got two cars," I answered, "and I just want to see what it's like."

Once again, in my quest to find myself, I'd thrown her and my family another curve ball without realizing how it might land on them.

But oh my, did I like this place right away!

The music was so upbeat, and they had dance teams, and the minster didn't wear a tie which was rare in those days. And he'd written a book about why he didn't wear a tie!

Everything about it was so exciting, contemporary, and very different from what I was used to coming from a traditional, Baptist church environment, that I got right into it.

Eva would come with me from time to time, but for the most part she wanted to stay with her conventional church setting and Sunday School. To some, Broadway was considered to be "a more aggressive church," and looking back I think maybe she wasn't wanting to make the change to be "more aggressive," or experience a different viewpoint about things.

Although I'd been raised to believe husbands and wives should go to church together, my attitude now, even if unintentional, was, "Well, she can come along or not!" For the first time since we'd left Lincoln, I'd found a spiritual community that really resonated with me and I could tell that the people were authentically joyous about celebrating their faith journey. It was a huge change from just "going to church," and exactly what I wanted and needed. At long last I'd found my path, and I just couldn't turn back.

Throughout my adult life I'd heard numerous horror stories of men who confided their sexual orientation to their ministers and were outed to the church, the deacon body, their families, and anyone else they could find. And I was terrified that could happen to me. But at Broadway, like our church experience in Lincoln, I felt comfortable revealing my history to one of the ministers, who later connected me with a therapist.

About a month later, after hearing about my life-long sexual identity struggles and destructive behaviors—the constant search for sex, watching tons of pornography, overeating, abusing alcohol and prescription drugs (which incidentally had started up again), and other things—all while trying, in some ways, to unravel my ties to the strict religious upbringing of my youth, my new therapist quickly recognized that addiction was my underlying issue.

So he introduced me to an organization called Sexaholics Anonymous (S.A. for short), a 12-Step recovery group based on the principles of A.A.

At the meetings there were men and women, gay and straight, young and old, and because it is non-denominational, like A.A., there were people of different races and faiths. So not only did I get to know these people's struggles, I also learned a lot about their "walk" and their faith traditions. S.A., I say, is where my eyes were really opened to the idea that there's more than one "church" in town. It was like nothing I'd ever experienced before in my life.

At every meeting we read aloud the organization's 12 steps (also adapted from A.A.), which basically state that we've become powerless over the cravings of lust and sexual activity and that we're turning it over to God (or whatever we called our Higher Power) for help, clarity, wisdom, and the strength to right the wrongs and hurt we've done in the past to ourselves and others.

"Yes! This is it!" I remember thinking. "These people really understand what I'm going through and it's going to be great – 12 steps, 12 meetings, and I'm outta here! I'll finally be healed, the addictive behaviors and 'gay thing' will be gone, and my family and I could live a normal life like everybody else; the life I've always wanted," my naïve mind said to me.

After a few meetings, however, I realized I had a lot more inner work to do.

One of the most important things I learned in S.A. is that sexually addictive behaviors are universal. And that straight men, whether single or married, often struggle with lustful thoughts about women. It's just that gay and straight people act out differently.

I also learned that I wasn't the only gay man thinking I could be fixed. Or that if I slept with a woman it could change things. So many others in S.A. had been down that road already and learned those things just weren't true.

At some point along the way I also joined a men's support group at Broadway. And oddly enough, just like my church support group in Lincoln, I was the only gay person in it. Most of the men here also knew Eva and what we were going through and were nothing but very supportive of us. And they all believed I could be healed from this form of addiction.

I had been brought up to believe that grace is given by God. But it wasn't until I got involved with these two groups that I realized we all have grace to give and can be open and willing to receive it.

The wonderful thing is that between Broadway and S.A. I'd found two new "spiritual homes." And with each passing day I established more friendships and was coming around to understanding so much more about myself.

At the same time, however, the gap in my marriage (whatever there was left of it) just kept getting wider, and wider.

I was still having sex with men on the side and had no idea how to stop it. However, I felt like I was getting to experience the real me. So although my internal chaos and physical and emotional distance from Eva continued to be a strain, like finding my spiritual path, I just couldn't turn back.

And although Eva wasn't happy, she wasn't willing to go to therapy this time—either with me or by herself—beyond the first few appointments. But anyone who has ever been in therapy knows the honeymoon is over after about three visits. That's when it's time to start really looking at your own stuff.

Bless her heart, I think she just had so much fear and hurt around not knowing what was going to happen if we finally acknowledged I was gay, and that our marriage and the outside-looking-in-picture-perfect-two-kids-and-a-white-picket-fence family life was over.

By now, David was enrolled as a student at Missouri State University in Springfield, MO, and Beth had graduated from Southwest Baptist University in Bolivar, MO, married a wonderful man named Brian, and moved to Bloomington, Ill.

About a decade later, David married as well to a woman named Jennifer, and in the process became an instant father to her two young sons—Nick and Cody—and Eva and I were thrilled to have what we called our "Bonus Grandsons."

As an empty-nester couple, Eva and I continued on like ships passing in the night. And when I couldn't take the stress and secrecy of my double life anymore, I made up my mind that I was going to have to leave.

When we finally separated, selling the house as well, I thought, "I'm going to give this a year to see what happens. Maybe we can work out something."

But our relationship, even from a distance, just kept getting worse. The oddly ironic part was that although things between us were progressively deteriorating, other parts of my life were getting better. Like I said before, I'd found stability at Broadway, established trusted friendships, and going to S.A.

and therapy really seemed to be helping me put my life into perspective.

Maybe, just maybe, if I could get things turned around (which meant not being gay anymore), Eva and I could get back together.

Chapter 12
All the Affirming in the World Wouldn't Change Me

For the most part, the spiritual side of my life was going pretty well.

My therapist and I were making great progress, S.A. was continuing to help me unravel my addictive behaviors, and the services and men's group at Broadway were still important parts of my healing work.

I was still in the process of learning to love myself.

Like I said before, one of the things that drew me to Broadway was that although most of the congregants were straight, they were very open to whomever worshipped there, and they continued to pray for my total healing.

Then the rug got pulled out from under me.

It was announced that they were becoming "gay affirming"—a place that doesn't consider homosexuality to be a sin against the church or God, and welcomes all Lesbian, Gay, Bisexual, Transgender, Questioning and Asexual (LGBTQA) people.

What?! All this time they were praying for me NOT to be gay, but now they're saying that gay is OK?

I was so angry, frustrated, disillusioned, and felt like I'd been duped. I thought I was on the brink of healing and living a "normal life," but no – it had all been a lie?

So I left, mad as hell and I was never coming back.

For the next 2 or 3 years I wandered around, searching for "the church"— that special spiritual home to call my own—one that was Baptist but leaned a little closer to something like Broadway with their livelier music and more progressive teachings. My experience at Broadway was so hurtful and disappointing that I definitely didn't want to go through that again.

While trying to sort all of this out, I also kept looking for "a tribe" at the local gay hangouts. Sure, I found plenty of action, but I was still running scared from my own low self-esteem and other issues.

By that time I'd changed therapists, and at one of my sessions along the way it was pointed out to me that I probably wasn't going to find spiritual fulfillment in bars. So he referred me to Spirit of Hope Metropolitan Community Church (MCC).

Although they weren't a Baptist church, they seemed to have the other two things I was looking for. And they were a predominantly gay church. But I still wanted to learn a little bit more about them first.

Because I was still so closeted and fearful of being found out, I went to a pay phone (remember those?) to call the church and ask questions about the services because I didn't want any connection between my home phone number (a landline, remember those too?) and them.

Satisfied with the answers I received and everything else I learned, I decided to check them out.

One Sunday I drove over there, parked a block away so my car wouldn't be seen by anybody, and watched "those gay people" go into that "gay church" before driving off. This happened three more Sundays before I was really ready to step inside (I found out later that a lot of people did that; afraid someone would see them, or afraid of the unknown. Or both).

The day I finally decided to "go all the way," I purposely arrived late and sat in the back row.

Then the song in the air pierced me like an arrow.

It was by a young man, who seemed to be gay, singing a solo about the challenges of life, and about being who you are – no matter what. It was as if he was telling my story, and just what I needed to hear.

During that same visit, closer to the front of the church, I saw this lady with a huge hat wearing a white suit; her hands in the air, totally enjoying herself. I was so drawn to her energy and just knew I needed to be surrounded by it.

When church was over, I made a quick move toward the exit, shook the minister's hand, thanked him for the service, did a quick surveillance up and down the street for anyone I might know, then ran to my car.

At this point, paranoia was my constant companion.

The next week, I arrived early so I could sit in the row behind that lady with the big hat, who when she noticed I was there introduced herself as Momma Charlie. She had a beautiful face and a big welcoming smile, and I just felt this warmth and loving energy radiating all around her.

Momma Charlie and so many others at that church, it seemed, were so comfortable expressing themselves as gay people. They weren't hesitant to hug, or kiss, or hold hands in front of anyone else. They were just relaxed and themselves.

What I really liked about the Sunday lessons at MCC was that they centered around hope, peace, forgiveness, and God's love for all creation. And when they read scriptures like John 3:16-17, for example—*For God so loved the world, that He gave his only begotten Son, that whoever believes in Him shall not perish, but have eternal life; For God did not send the Son into the world to judge the world, but that the world might be saved through Him*—it was one of the first times in my adult life I really understood that there were no asterisks to exclude anybody.

Even if the "outside world" was not accepting of homosexuality, I could see that MCC was a safe haven, a sanctuary where I could just be me with no fear of harm or being found out.

* * *

A few years later "on the Baptist side of the street," the word was out: The minister at Broadway had gotten divorced from his wife … and he was gay.

I wasn't really surprised by this news, as his demeanor was always very effeminate. But beyond that, maybe the whole thing about changing to an LGBTQA affirming church had a lot to do with his own "healing" toward living an authentic life too.

I guess you could say that when I was a member there, I was as "spiritually two-faced" as they were. I mean, on Saturday nights I'd be just a couple of blocks away picking up guys in a bar, then going back to church on Sunday morning to ask for a healing. Yet I'd left in anger because I believed they weren't being truthful.

Now coming from a healthier place in my life, I realized that the people at Broadway never actually said, or suggested, that the healing we prayed for was specifically to "make me straight." That was my own distorted interpretation of what I wanted to hear and have happen.

Sometime later I went back to Broadway for an event, and the minister happened to be there. When he saw me, without hesitation he walked right over and embraced me. And in that hug, I could feel the warmth of oneness between us.

I apologized for how I behaved before and told him I was starting to feel more comfortable with who I was.

I can only imagine that God was happy that I'd cleaned all of that up and that two of his children had finally come together in love. It brought to mind the song "God Danced the Day You were Born," where the lyrics talk about God and the angels dancing; movin' and groovin' in unbridled joy that I had made my appearance on this earth. I was a gift they were glad to share with the world.

Knowing in my heart that my Creator loves and accepts me unconditionally, let's me know that I am more than enough.

All the affirming in the world wouldn't change me.

God danced the day I was born, and the dancing hasn't stopped since!

Chapter 13
<u>"You shall know the truth,
and the truth will set you free."</u>

The word "freedom" has a lot of meanings, and we all decide how we want to interpret it.

At different times throughout my self-discovery journey, John 8:32 from the Bible came to mind which says, "You shall know the truth, and the truth shall set you free." I interpreted that to mean I was going to find out what caused me to be gay, I was going to be set free from it, and it wouldn't *ever* happen again.

But after moving from Princeton to Lincoln, Dahlonega, and then to Kansas City, experiencing different church communities in each place, getting into therapy, and becoming involved with several different groups, I just couldn't reconcile, "You shall know the truth" with, "But I'm not healed yet!"

One day during a session with my therapist I blurted out, "I need to talk to you about something ... about these things we've discussed. I've been coming to you for years, and I'm as gay as the day I walked in here. So, I'm going to have to drop out and find my own way on this."

"Oh no, John! Don't do that! We are so close!" he said. "You've just about got it. Stay with me. Stay with me!"

"Well then tell me what I need to do."

He kind of danced around it, and kept coming back to, "Stay with me."

"No, tell me what to do."

After more dancing I said again, "No! Tell me what to do!"

Now speechless, he just sat there. After a few moments he finally said, "I don't know."

If neither of us had the answer, there was no reason for me to keep coming in. So, I thanked him for all of his time, attention, and care, and paid my final bill.

Right before I left, he told me to feel free to come back any time.

For a while I was content to just be me—whoever that was— and not try to figure out what to do. But about two months later I realized I really needed someone to talk to, so I found another new therapist. A few appointments in, the rubber started to hit the road.

"What do you want?" he repeatedly asked me.

"I want to be straight! I want to be straight! If I can be straight, I want to stay married."

"How will you know when you are straight?"

I'd already thought about it and all I could say was, "Well, I just don't know how to do that."

"This is what I want you to do," he said. "Every time you see a woman that turns you on, describe her a little bit on a piece of paper and what you felt was so attractive about her. And every time you see a man that turns you on, do the same thing. Then we can compare notes and see where you might be."

I agreed, wanting to grasp onto anything in my desperation that could help me "be straight."

But in the back of my mind I was pretty sure these would be two very lopsided lists.

Chapter 14
<u>There's a Vagina in the Hot Tub</u>

I used to be a member at a former health club at the Adams Mark Hotel just east of downtown Kansas City. One day after a workout session, I decided to have a soak in the hot tub. While walking toward it, I noticed this really good-looking man sitting in the water. Not long after I stepped down into it, he and I struck up a conversation.

In my head, with my sexually addictive behavior, I come up with, *Oh! I think he kinda likes me!* And I felt like he started lighting up, and he was smiling more, and I'm like, *Wow!* And my mind is just getting all crazy with it.

Then I hear a woman's voice behind me, and he says to her, "Honey, there are steps over here for you."

In that instant, his conversation with me was over.

I don't know if the woman was his girlfriend or wife, but it didn't matter. He wasn't looking or thinking about me at all! His sights were clearly set on her, and this whole hot and steamy love scene I'd created in my mind was just a foolish, lustful daydream.

Adding insult to injury, for the next several minutes, as if I wasn't even there, the two of them proceeded to play huggy-bear-kissy-face, totally oblivious to the self-inflicted shame and disappointment I was now soaking in – at 105 degrees no less.

When nature called, I assume, the woman got up to leave the hot tub. And when she stepped up onto the bench seat to get out the wet clinging part at the bottom of her swimsuit moved to one side, and I caught of glimpse of her vagina.

So here I am, only seeing this guy from the neck up, and I'm so hot the water is bubbling on its own. But when I see a woman with her feminine parts in full view – there's no reaction whatsoever. She might as well have shown me her ear, I was so non-affected by what I saw.

"OK," I thought. "Of all the notes I've made for my therapy homework assignments, there have been plenty about men (my heavy attraction to those with olive complexions, deep southern accents, "dancing eyes," a cute ass …) but none for women. It's pretty obvious that I don't need to make any more lists."

When I went to my next appointment, I told the therapist all about the hot tub incident and my note taking experiences.

"So, what do you want to do?" he asked.

Still not ready to fully embrace being gay I said, "Let's give it a year without me trying to change things and see how that works."

Chapter 15
<u>When the Marbles Hit the Stairs</u>

The first strange symptoms I remember having were a little bit of nausea and lots of very active, smelly, discolored stools, which was definitely abnormal. And then some friends commented that I looked kind of "yellow." I knew something wasn't right, but just thought it was the flu.

"I'll go to the doctor, get a few shots or something, and then I'll be as good as new again," I said to myself.

After an examination and some routine bloodwork, my general practitioner said he was sending me to another doctor.

About two weeks later after that new doctor visit, I was sent to get an MRI. As they were laying me down to move into the big, tubular machine I thought, "They don't do this for the flu."

Looking at the technician I said, "It sounds to me like they're looking for cancer."

She didn't say a word, but that silence spoke volumes.

Another referral, this time to the oncology department and more blood tests followed. But even with that, my brain hadn't yet grasped onto the possibility of the "C word."

When the oncologist called that chilly afternoon in March, I was leaning up against my massage table, cup of coffee in hand, listening while he just kept going on and on and on.

Finally, I said, "OK, Doc. Bottom line. What are you telling me?" In my head I'm thinking, "Come on man, it's Friday. I've got weekend plans!"

"Well," he said, "We found cancer. It's in your liver and lymph nodes."

That's when the first glass marbles started to fall down that cold, hard, concrete stairway.

Stage 4 Cancer.

       Inoperable.

          Incurable.

"There's nothing you can do?" I asked.

"Well, there is a treatment. But it's fairly new. We might be able to get you a couple of more months, but that treatment would cause nausea, constant diarrhea, and you wouldn't be feeling good."

              Terminal.

                 Irreparable.

He also said I could do chemo and radiation, but he didn't think a lot of results would come of it. And it could kill me.

Fatal.

Lethal.

"Or your quality of life would really go down and you could spend your last two months in the hospital. Take some time to think about it."

Six-to-eight months to live.

I'm so sorry, John.

After I got off the phone, I just stood there thinking about what he'd said and the disbelief of it all. And then I thought, "Oh my God! My hair is going to fall out!"

Now you know you're a gay man if the doctor says you're dying and one of the first things that comes to mind is that you're going to lose your hair! At least my strange sense of humor was still intact, even if for just a few moments.

At that point, my two choices were: Try this new treatment and risk an even earlier death or spend the last two months of my life languishing away in some hospital bed.

Bang.
Bang.

Bang.

    Bang.

        Bang.

            Bang.

                Bang.

                    Bang.

                        Bang.

                            Bang.

                                Bang.

It was like a waterfall of marbles making its way down to a body of water below.

There was nothing to do at that point but go back out to my garden and keep digging. Those tulip and daffodil bulbs still had a chance to bloom, even if I might not be here to see them.

* * *

After Bill left, I called my son, David, to give him the news. It broke my heart to hear him just cry, and cry, and cry.

"Even dogs have a better life than that, Dad!" he blurted out between sobs.

Beth beat me to the punch, calling just to ask about the results of the routine tests she knew I'd taken. When I told her what the doctor said, I'm sure she felt her own marbles crashing to the floor. Both of us spent most of that phone call crying.

Later that night, David and my grandson, Robby, came over. When I opened the door, I got what I'd call a "Golden Girls hug." Then we just sat on the sofa, one on each side of me; nobody saying a word. Just having them there is what I really, really needed.

When I started making calls to tell the rest of my family, their reactions were pretty much the same. I'm sure the marbles were hitting the stairs for them as well. Shock. Anger. Here we go again—another Delameter is going to die. One of my sisters cried out, "Oh that cancer is going to get all of us!"

When Beth arrived a few days later from Illinois, the first thing she said was, "Tell me what you need dad. Your daughter is going to get it for you."

After all those years of taking care of them, they were now there to take care of *me.*

Instead of trying to repeat every detail of what I'd been told, and to give them a better sense of the diagnosis and different treatment options, I decided to take each one of them with me, individually, to see the oncologist. I hadn't really thought about it ahead of time but listening to the bad news in its dire entirety two more times was starting to make me feel numb.

Reality was settling in, and I was slowly starting to feel the gravity of it all.

After our meetings with the doctor, both kids said I should do whatever I felt was the right thing for me, and they would honor that. "It's your life, it's your body, and we want you to be happy," was the message of love they conveyed.

Although I tried to put on a brave face for everybody, most of the time I felt wrung out and rundown. I always had an upset stomach, and the diarrhea and jaundice were still there. I never really experienced sleepless nights however, I would sometimes wake up and say to myself, "That was me the doctor called to say I had cancer! Not my neighbor. Not a sibling. Not a coworker. It was ME, it was real, and it did happen."

Emotionally I was completely overwhelmed and not thinking there was any hope for me, so there was probably no reason to put myself through trial drugs, or chemo, or radiation. It would just delay the fast approaching inevitable.

Despite this I did believe that somehow God had me, and there was some small ray of hope that I would live.

Chapter 16
<u>The Law of Attraction</u>

There are different ways to explain the Law of Attraction, the spiritual law and ability to attract—consciously or unconsciously—into our lives whatever we focus on. And while I certainly wasn't focused on a cancer diagnosis, I was walking around completely unconscious to how deeply my old stories were manifesting in my body.

Cancer didn't just land on me. I invited it in.

***

Studies have shown that an unborn child can detect what's going on in their soon-to-be outer world. I believe that to be very true in my life.

For starters, my parents were gripped by fear surrounding World War II and the fact that my oldest brother, H.A., was not only the first child out of the nest but shipped off somewhere in the South Pacific to fight for our country.

Their decision to have a child to take their mind off of all of this was not quite what they bargained for. Hoping for another girl whose name was to be "Judy," they got a boy instead. All my life I kept hearing family members repeat this story, and I'm sure that on some subconscious level I assumed it meant I wasn't really what they wanted, I was a disappointment, not good enough, and there wasn't enough room for me.

I was three months old when my nephew Ellis, H.A.'s son, was born. My parents' first grandchild.

It's kind of strange, but even at that young age I felt like suddenly my mommy and daddy had somebody more special than me. This special baby's daddy had left for the war, and they weren't going to see him for a few years - if they ever got to see him again at all. Now that I'm a grandparent, I understand that extra special feeling we get with our grandbabies. But at the time, within my undeveloped consciousness, I misinterpreted the abundance of touching and holding going on with Ellis as a lack of it for me.

The truth is that my parents never set out to reject me; to make me feel abandoned. Nevertheless, as Ellis and I grew up my misguided feelings toward him and my parents continued.

Since we were both raised in the same community, he and I and my younger brother Jerrie did a lot of fun things together: splashing around in the local ponds and creeks, mushroom hunting, participating in church activities, goofing around at family gatherings, and the like. Years later when Eva and I married, I was so proud to have him beside me as one of my groomsmen.

But underneath all of this great friendship and mutual admiration I still felt, though it was never implied, stated, or demonstrated, that I was second class; that same feeling I had when we were taken from our one-room schoolhouse in the country and shuttled to the bigger school in town.

100

I was allowed to be there, but I felt like I wasn't really wanted. And it didn't help my victimhood story that neither I, nor Jerrie, nor my sister Jo, had grandparents to dote on us growing up. All of them passed away during our elementary school years.

Ellis, on the other hand, had all four—my mom and dad and H.A.'s in-laws—and a great grandmother to boot!

Back then, in my immature mind, there also seemed to be a lot of "evidence" that I should have been a girl.

In addition to my parents choosing the name "Judy" for their unborn child, when I did come into this world as a boy, I became Johnnie: J-O-H-N-N-I-E. When people misspelled it with a "y" at the end and I'd correct them, saying it should be "i-e," they'd say, "Well, that's how a girl would spell it!"

Thinking about it now, I'm not even sure that spelling was intentional. Maybe the doctor accidentally wrote it down like that on my birth certificate, sent it in to the county recorder, and my parents never even knew it was misspelled until much later on.

It's funny because not until I was writing this book did I realize that although Jerrie's name is also spelled very differently than what you typically see for a boy—J-E-R-R-I-E—it never once occurred to me that someone might think that was "evidence" that he should have been a girl as well (and I wonder if he ever got teased about it, like I did). Jerrie might have been many things, but feminine he was not!

But it probably wouldn't have mattered, because my mindset was on all of the things that were wrong with me.

Around the time that most boys' voices changed, getting deeper, mine had not.

I was overweight and my chest was larger than the other boys, so that meant I had boobs.

And I liked doing things that girls liked to do.

For example, when no one was looking I'd put on my mother's clothing. One of my favorite pieces was her long, elegant fur coat which looked great on me and made my whole-body tingle. And to complete the ensemble, I'd put on her sparkly rhinestone necklace (only after 6:00 p.m., of course!). To this day I still remember how good it felt to slip my feet into her suede, opened-toed, 2-inch heels. Looking back I have to wonder, even at only age 8 or 9 if I was one of Mercer County's first drag queens!

As a little side tale, years later a friend and I were sharing childhood dress-up stories and he told me one about cutting some jeans off real short, making a crop top out of his t-shirt, wearing his sister's majorette boots, and twirling a baton around in the front yard. At that same moment, his father's carpool came by to bring him home from work, and as you might imagine what they were seeing didn't go over very well. My friend just thought what he was doing was normal, like every boy did that kind of thing, as I did with dressing up in Mother's clothes.

And to top it all off, I feared that someday my mother was going to come to me and say we had to go to the doctor for surgery to officially turn me into a girl.

That fear seemed like it was about to come true when my mother actually did pull me aside one day, explaining that when I was born the doctor "was supposed to do a surgery on me" but he didn't. So during one of our trips to his office for a check-up, I might have to have it done.

Just as she began telling me this, the neighbors turned into our driveway and our conversation was cut short. So I lived with this fear that I'd one day become Judy after all.

You may have guessed it already, but the "surgery" the doctor hadn't performed was my circumcision. I never knew why he didn't do it when I was a baby, or why mother never made sure it happened during my one of pediatric check-ups. But once I was in high school and started taking showers after gym class, I realized that only me and one other boy were uncircumcised, and that was very, very embarrassing for me.

It wasn't long before I realized the whole sex change thing was a big, dramatic story I'd made up in my mind that wasn't ever going to happen.

But as they say, there is a blessing in everything.

Once I entered the gay world as an adult, I learned that when looking for a partner, or husband, or whatever, being "UC"— Uncut—is highly sought-after and a great marketing tool!

Many men seek out UC's because (now don't faint, siblings, kids, and grandkids) when having sex it just feels different. Apparently, a very small percentage of men my age are UC's so I'm a hot commodity now!

But in all seriousness, the subconscious stories I'd made up about all of these childhood events were, over time, just marinating and settling into every cavity of my mind, body, and spirit. It was like a pot sitting on a low flame where the individual ingredients would eventually create a thick, meaty stew.

Many years later, once it was revealed that my wife had a gay husband, my kids a gay dad, and my siblings a gay brother, and Eva and I were on the brink of divorce, and things were just so crazy, I remember thinking things like:

"I bet if I died nobody would even care!"

"I'm not good enough and nobody wants me, so I might as well die. Nobody would notice."

"What would happen if I just vanished off the face of the earth?"

That "not good enough," "second class," "nobody gets me" stew was being dished out with a huge ladle and everyone—including me—was feasting on it.

But wait, there's more!

Every August, we have a big family reunion in Princeton. That particular year when things with my family were so all over the place, and I was feeling like an utter failure, I was too ashamed and embarrassed to go. So, not only did I not show up, I didn't even bother calling anyone to say I wasn't coming.

I went to church instead, then to an S.A. meeting, then home to check and see who'd called to find out what was wrong since I hadn't shown up at the reunion.

Nobody had called.

About a week later, however, I got a card from a niece who said she hoped I was OK and that she missed and loved me.

Despite her beautiful words, in my troubled mind my inner dialogue was still:

"You see? They don't like me."

"Nobody really cares or missed me."

"I could have been in an accident and because no one called, they wouldn't have known."

"I might as well be dead."

And I kept repeating those things, replaying them in my head and wallowing in that old unwanted and unloved childhood story, with more and more "evidence" (like no one calling to check on me) showing up to support my beliefs.

The icing on that low self-worth cake was thick with still trying to figure out what was wrong with me and how to "fix it."

I didn't know it at the time that I was fully exercising the Law of Attraction, but unfortunately to my detriment.

All of it, I truly believe, came together, and showed up as cancer.

Chapter 17
<u>Richard</u>

Richard Fawcett and I met in the early 2000s. My friend Bill had been going to him off and on for years and was so happy with the way he was helping him with issues in his life, Bill thought we might be a good match as well.

Richard turned out to be one of the greatest teachers my soul has ever known.

His life is a fascinating read and I think he should write a book about it!

As Richard tells it, his road to becoming a spiritual counselor, spiritual healer, and minister was full of unexpected and exciting twists and turns.

After graduating from the University of Minnesota in 1959 with Bachelor of Arts degrees in Speech and English, followed by a master's degree in Speech in 1966, he went on to teach both at the high school level.

His first formal introduction to religion was a course on comparative religions taught at Macalester College in St. Paul, MN by the late Dr. Yahya Armajani, (for those of you who are old enough, some of his students include people like former Vice President Walter Mondale, and the late Ghanaian diplomat Kofi Annan).

What first struck him about Dr. Armajani was when he spoke about any world religion, he did so as if talking about *his own* religious affiliation and personal connection. Richard said it was such an eye opener to the Spirit, or a higher power, that exists in us all.

Exposure to meditation by Dr. Usharbudh Arya from India, and the late Dainin Katagiri, an author and Zen meditation master affiliated with both the Minnesota Monterey and San Francisco Zen Meditation Centers also influenced Richard's life. So much so that he's been an active meditator since 1968 - now meditating between 1-1½ hours every day.

Richard also learned about Socratic Inquiry—named after Greek philosopher Socrates—a process of questioning based on thoughtful, disciplined dialogue. He was so moved by all of these teachings that in the late '90s he became a minister ordained by the Alliance of Divine Love, an international interfaith ministry founded to study and share the concept of love in all religions and to support, as their website states, "those seeking to awaken to their higher consciousness as they are divinely guided."

A training certification through Core Star, Inc., an organization that promotes self-healing and well-being by using our own human energy fields (most people call them our "Chakras" or "Auric Field") was also part of Richard's educational experience.

Whew! So, what does any of this have to do with my Stage 4 cancer diagnosis? It does in more ways than I could have possibly imagined.

Sometime in the 1980s, Richard found himself suffering from Irritable Bowel Syndrome, and a hiatal hernia, which happens when part of the stomach bulges and pushes up through the diaphragm.

For months he tried alleviating his pain with traditional, doctor-prescribed medications, but it didn't help.

After a while he heard about a Native American healer who specialized in pain relief without the use of drugs. After describing his symptoms, her first thought was that Richard might have a milk allergy.

"So, she takes my non-dominant arm and extends it straight out in front of me," Richard explained, "puts two fingers on my wrist, and says, 'This body can tolerate milk products.' And whew! My arm just fell right down to my side," indicating, according to the healer, that this was a false statement. If she'd said his body could *not* tolerate milk products, his arm would have remained firm.

Looking back later at his childhood, Richard remembered being fed a special formula because his body couldn't tolerate regular milk.

"After my visit with the healer I stopped drinking milk and eating lactose products immediately, and within two or three weeks all my symptoms disappeared! How the healer knew this was the possible culprit I have no idea. But the experience, in addition to my previous energy field, spiritual healing, and meditation work convinced me at a much higher level that there was so much more to the function of the physical body than we knew."

Drawing on this and his other past experiences, Richard explained to me that the body has a lot to say, IF we just listen. And "The body doesn't lie."

Richard and I only had about two or three sessions together. Despite his personal and professional experiences and enthusiasm for more spiritual and intuitive ways to heal the body, these concepts seemed pretty far out there to me, and weren't something I felt I needed.

Five years would pass before I came back to see him.

Chapter 18
<u>Getting Pushed from the Nest</u>

Parenting a teen or young adult is a lot like a bird raising chicks – at some point they may have to be pushed from the nest.

The intention for both is about the same - moving our young into independence by allowing (or forcing) them to spread their wings and fly. Either species may run into problems, like hitting the ground and getting injured at first. But the hope is that they will eventually go out into the world and make their own way.

Taking flight toward complete ownership of my thoughts, words, and actions, and in time fully embracing my sexuality however, required an abrupt and somewhat painful shove.

It happened the day my boss came into my work area and said, "Did you know that an officer from the Sheriff's office is downstairs and they want to serve papers on you?"

"What for?" I asked, completely confused.

"Well," he said, "It's probably divorce papers."

My mind was whirling. How could that be? Eva and I had recently been to counseling where she'd said that if "this" (well, really, if "I") could be fixed, she wanted to stay married.

"There's a coffee room that's vacant right now and he's in there," my boss said, interrupting my thoughts. "Now John," he continued, "I just want to encourage you to go down, don't make a scene, and do whatever has to be done. And if you want to leave for a while that's fine. Just let me know whatever it is you need to do."

After gathering myself a bit I went down to the coffee room, signed the paperwork, and watched the Sheriff walk out.

My mind, whirling again, came up with, "Well, this is kind of what I wanted, but I wasn't really expecting it."

After taking a quick look at the papers inside the envelope, I trudged across the street to Eva's office and sat down in a chair in front of her desk.

Filled with mixed emotions I said, "Why did you do this?"

"Well, they thought I should," she responded, "they" being other people she always relied upon to tell her what to do. It was a rare event when she made a decision on her own.

"I thought we said we were going to try and work on this," I went on, "and if we decided to move ahead with a divorce to use one attorney."

"Well, no, I've been advised not to get just one attorney," she said.

Not knowing what else to do I simply said, "Well, OK, if this is what you want," and I walked back across the street.

A bit later my boss came by again to see what happened. I shared how I was kind of shocked about the whole thing and thanked him for being so compassionate. If he hadn't given me a heads up, I would've been completely blindsided walking into something like that.

"Yeah, but something else happened that you need to know about," he said. "Your wife was very upset that you came over and talked to her, so we're going to ask you not to go by her desk again."

"Well, then how are we going to work this out?" I asked.

"I don't know John. But I know that if you continue to meet, one of you is going to go off the deep end, and there will be a big scene and a big ugly mess here at work, and we will not have that. So, the best thing to do is to not communicate at work at all."

Although I'd been living in a pretty uncomfortable nest all of these years, this big shove toward the edge was a necessary one.

For the next few years, Eva and I somehow managed to keep things civil at the office, and eventually our divorce was final.

Evidence that I was still somewhat falling and hadn't yet fully spread my wings came several years later when I started experiencing some flu-like symptoms. Catching the flu was very unusual for me and these symptoms lasted for several days.

When the weekend rolled around, I was still sick, but I'd already planned for my kids and grandkids to come over for a visit. I was so excited about it and didn't want to cancel, so I ordered and had a big dinner delivered, and hoped we'd still get to do at least some of the fun things I had in mind. But by the time they arrived I could hardly get out of bed. I did somehow manage to pull myself together enough to sit with them and eat a little bit, but after they left, I was so weak I went right back to bed.

The next Monday, although still not feeling well, I went to work and shared this experience with a co-worker who said, "Well John, you got sick because Eva got remarried this past weekend."

"Now what in the world does that have to do with anything!" I responded, somewhat shocked.

"Eva was your high school sweetheart," he said gently. "You two were going to spend the rest of your lives together. But now that door has been permanently closed."

Once the words left his lips I realized that in trying to make everything perfect for my kids' and grandkids' visit, which was right after Eva's wedding, and to show them I was OK with it, I'd been pushing down my feelings about the fact she and I hadn't been able to work things out. And now it was too late.

The interesting thing is, once I realized this, I immediately started feeling better. And within a day or two the flu-like symptoms had completely disappeared. It was just like what Richard said about our bodies talking to us. Despite wanting and getting a divorce, my subconscious mind was apparently still hoping for a reconciliation. I'd been holding all of that in my body since the divorce papers were signed, but now it was time to let it go.

* * *

After almost two decades with the Nazarene Publishing House and working for some 45 years of my life overall, it was time to start planning my retirement. Beth and David were healthy and happy, living their own separate lives, so it was time for me to turn the page to my next chapter.

It was going to be a little bit of an early retirement at age 62, but I knew that my pension would cover my living expenses just fine until social security kicked in three years later. However, there would be a $300 a month gap I'd need to fill during that time to help cover the full cost of my health insurance.

I really didn't want to get a part time job or launch into a new career where it might take years for me to establish myself. So I tried out a few freelance jobs on the side. But the thing I just loved doing, dating back to my childhood, was working with plants and flowers!

I knew my green thumb was a good start, but not enough to help the general public. So I took some flower arranging classes and decided to go ahead and take a part-time job at a local flower shop working evenings, weekends, and holidays.

I loved it - the creativity of flower arranging and working with people. It was so gratifying to help some little guy who came in to get a corsage, or some little girl who wanted to buy a boutonniere for prom night. The flower they choose may have been nothing but a white carnation, but to them it was a sparkle in their eye and the promise of a beautiful evening.

One of my funniest experiences was with a 16 or 17-year old who came in on Valentine's Day to buy two flower arrangements. As I was pulling them together, I said, "Somebody's going to have a very happy mother and a very happy girlfriend!" But that wasn't it at all. "No, I have two girlfriends," he said, then proceeded to take his time writing out a special card for each of his love interests!

Creating floral arrangements for weddings was one of my favorite tasks. It was so wonderful to work late on a Friday night to get things just right, then deliver them to the delighted wedding party on Saturday morning and help make the church or whatever venue look so beautiful.

For any of these events those flowers, and the pictures they took, would be something they'd have and remember for years and years to come.

I also worked with grieving families who came in for special floral arrangements to celebrate the lives of their loved ones.

One client's mother, who I knew and was very fond of, was known for her apple growing and pies, and the family wanted something to symbolize and honor that passion on her casket.

Trying to come up with something they might like, I went into the back of the shop and found four plastic apples I thought I could incorporate into the memorial spray. They were ecstatic because there were four kids in the family and the apples could represent each one of them!

During the gathering after the funeral, so many people shared how appreciative they were of the thought and care I put into that design.

I really felt for all of my customers and put as much love, compassion, and support as I could into my creations. I really enjoyed being part of these people's lives and able to serve them in that way.

Nevertheless, as exciting and meaningful as my flower arranging was, it just wasn't enough money to help support me. The only way I was ever going to make any money there would be to buy the shop. But if I were going to do that, which would have been a full-time job, I might as well stay where I was at the publishing house for several more years!

It was finally time to leave everything from my former nest, spread my wings, and fly.

Dr. Martin Luther King, Jr. once said, "Take the first step in faith. You don't have to see the whole staircase, just take the first step."

Although I didn't know what my next step would be, I knew that somehow it would lead me to greater levels of living my true and authentic self.

Chapter 19
The Energy of Life

Right around the time I was thinking about leaving the flower shop in search of a better paying, soon-to-be post-retirement, part-time job, a friend mentioned a massage class he was getting ready to take. An introductory weekend workshop was coming up and it wasn't very expensive.

The idea kind of appealed to me but I didn't know much about massage. So I decided to pay the fee and join him.

One of the things I learned is that there's a lot more that goes into massage than the actual physical strokes of one's hands. It also involves connecting with the emotional body, and how to make it a very spiritual experience for the client as well as the massage therapist.

That was a real eye-opener. Until that point in my life, connecting with someone through physical touch was something I'd been missing—both giving and receiving. It wasn't about lust, or even sex, but connecting with someone on a level that was, literally, more than skin deep.

To help us get a sense of what a career as a massage therapist might be like, the attendees tried some massage work on each other. I distinctly remember standing there, putting my hands on another person's back, and just feeling the electricity of the body which I now know as energy. In that moment I knew this was a path I needed and wanted to pursue.

At the end of the introductory weekend, I dove right in to finding massage training schools, eventually choosing one of the only three in town at the time.

For the next three years my evenings and weekends would be taken up with classes and lots of studying at home in order to get my certification. And I got lucky, because the publishing house provided up to $2,000 a year in tuition reimbursement for continuing education to its employees, so that potential obstacle was off my mind!

Nevertheless, as excited as I was to get started along this new career path, there were a few unexpected mental and emotional struggles that came up.

For one, after a full day at the publishing house my co-workers got to go home to their families for dinner, play with their kids, and spend time with their spouses or partners. I, on the other hand, had to hurry home in rush hour traffic, open and quickly gulp down a can of soup as my dinner, drive to the classes which were about 20 miles from my house, then drive home again to an empty home with nothing but the walls to greet me. Depending on the time of year and the weather, the drive could be painfully slow and even a little dangerous – and dark and/or cold to boot!

When summer rolled around, my friends were driving down to the lake on the weekends to escape the city and have some fun. But I was stuck taking additional classes to finish as soon as possible and start earning that extra income before I retired and had to rely on social security.

Despite this, I kept telling myself what football great Jerry Rice once said: "Today I will do what others won't, so tomorrow I can accomplish what others can't," and that mantra seemed to keep me going.

At some point near the beginning of the training there was a lady in my class who had a license plate that said "Healer." When I saw it, my early-in-life church background popped into my head, which said there was only one healer – and that was God. I knew that what I wanted to do was important, but I guess I hadn't realized in many was I was becoming a healer.

And it seemed like evidence of my natural gift and how I was really helping people kept showing up.

I remember a time once I'd reached the actual practice hours stage, when a man experiencing a lot of stress at his job came to see me. His shoulders were all slumped over as he dragged his body into the massage studio at my house, and he struggled to get up on the table.

Within about 20 minutes I could see that my hands and healing consciousness had taken root, and he'd just let go of everything. About an hour or so later after I'd finished and gone back into the living room to wait for him, out came this brand-new person! He was standing straight up, seemed so relaxed, and had a big smile on his face. It was so rewarding to be able to make a difference in his life like that, and to bring him back to a better state of physical health.

Then there was the time I had a client whose right ankle had been frozen up for years. It wouldn't move the way a healthy ankle did, and he couldn't walk very far because of the intense pain. Because this significantly decreased his mobility, if he was, for example, wanting to run errands in a strip mall-like area, he'd need to find a parking spot near his first stop, go in and take care of business, then get back in the car and drive a few hundred yards down the way to another parking spot, and so forth.

When I first started working on his ankle, I wasn't really sure how I was going to manipulate it without causing him more suffering. The best thing I could do alongside my therapeutic strokes was to focus on putting positive energy into every bone, tendon, tissue, and blood vessel.

About the third or fourth time he came to see me, while lying on his stomach with his foot up in the air as I was manipulating his ankle, it suddenly gave way. I don't know which one of us was more excited! In fact, I was so overjoyed that without thinking I started to lean forward to kiss his ankle in gratitude but backed away at the last moment as I realized that wouldn't be at all professional!

My client on the other hand teared up right away with the realization that his ankle, that for many years caused him to walk with a limp, that traditional doctors were unable to fix, had finally opened up and was free.

One of the most rewarding and fun parts of my training, however, was practicing massage on my grandchildren! When I brought my massage table to their house, they would hop up onto it and I'd show them how to properly drape someone at every point during a session. They were intrigued, wanting to know why I had to cover someone up at all (I'd forgotten that at that age, modesty is not a big deal!). So, I explained that our genitals are our private area, and we all have a right to decide who gets to see them.

"Mom and dad already told us that," they responded, and it felt so good to be able to balance out the teaching they were getting at home with why that part of my work was so important.

In addition to the hands-on techniques, our training included learning how to make a Chi ball. The word Chi (pronounced "chee") comes from Chinese medicine and refers to the life-force—the invisible energy believed to be within and around everything—that can be harnessed at any time.

The best way to describe this technique commonly used in mind-body exercise programs like yoga, meditation, Pilates, and other practices, is to visualize holding a ball between your hands and gently pushing them towards each other to keep the ball from falling to the ground. When I did this for the first time I could instantly feel this unmistakable, tangible energy that felt like heat, and was starting to understand how it could be used to help heal another person whether sending it to them energetically, or bathing their body with it through physical touch.

This Chi ball practice became such a powerful one for me that years later I had a client ask if I'd put my hands in the microwave to warm them up before touching her (Yes, she really did ask me that!).

The morning after we first tried this in class I went to church. And while singing with my hands up in the air, I all of a sudden felt that energy—that Chi vibration—pulsating between them.

Jokingly, I said to myself, "OK God. You know I'm trying to worship you here, and you want to play Chi ball!" And God said back to me, "Well it's my day, and it's my house, and I'll play ball if I want to!"

In that instant, the stern opinion of God I was raised with had transformed into a more loving, playful being that wasn't "out to get me" at every turn. We were instead co-creative partners in a mentally, spiritually, and emotionally healing experience.

In many ways I don't believe it's so much about creating positive energy, rather unearthing or tuning into it. I've explained this to people by comparing it to radio airwaves. When you turn the dial to a particular station, it comes in strong and clear because you tuned into its frequency. But if you are, for example, driving down the road, getting further and further away from where the signal is transmitted, the channel starts screeching, getting weaker, or cutting out altogether. To tune back into the frequency you have to readjust the dial.

The same goes for our physical bodies. The energy is there, and we can connect to it at any given moment.

The Chi ball work tied right into, again, what Richard had told me about how our bodies talk to us all the time. So, when something unsettling or painful is going on we need to stop and listen up!

If one of my clients was having an issue with their digestive system, I could move a Chi ball in the same direction as the natural flow of food and allow that positive flow of energy help clean, reuse, or get rid of any negative or stuck energy.

And I was using this practice on myself too. I'd get a little stiff neck, or something would be hurting, or there'd be times when my hands got a little sore, and I'd just make a Chi ball and massage those areas to clear the issue and "heal thyself."

There was a time several years ago when I volunteered to give chair massages at a local rodeo. The second morning of the event I woke up with intense pain in my lower back and was thinking, "Oh no! What am I going to do if I can hardly get out of bed?" So instead, I brought myself up to a sitting position, tapped into some positive energy by making a Chi ball, and changed my thoughts to, *I'm OK. I'm healthy. I'll be all right.*

As I stood up, I kept kind of waiting to feel the pain. But then I reminded myself again, "Don't look for the pain. Look for how good I feel." And before I knew it, everything was working just fine.

Like I said in the very beginning of this book, I'm not a doctor and would never tell someone not to seek out a medical professional. So please don't misunderstand what I'm saying to mean that we can cure any physical ailment with only positive thoughts. However, we can *always* give healing energy to it.

I've been in and out of the hospital for short periods of time at various times in my life, and definitely needed professional intervention. But while going through those challenges I didn't sit around talking about how bad I felt or get stuck on getting instant gratification through an immediate healing. I've seen that happen many times when visiting people in the hospital, at a rest home, or in some other similar scenario where everyone is complaining about their health and you can just feel the energy in the room going down. That kind of attitude and negative talk just invites in more illness – and their cousins too!

Over the years I've had a number of people come to me with some pretty severe things their doctors wanted to cure with surgery. And again, I would never discourage anyone from seeing a medical professional. However, I have been able to help by showing them how to create positive thoughts, which in turn can open channels to better health (money, relationships, meaningful work...) and overall wellness. It's about giving the Universe (or God, Spirit, whatever you call your Higher Presence) *permission* to co-create with you. I believe that's when real healing begins.

As I progressed toward achieving higher and higher frequency levels in every area of my life, I continued to feel completely and totally free to enjoy the work I was doing.

Now of course, because I'm human, there are those times when I catch myself drifting off the path, perhaps saying or thinking something like, "I need an extra $500 by the end of the month to pay the rent." Well, the Universe has no numbers or timeline to It. I just need to get clear on what I need and be open to how it shows up. I'll often say to God, "I ask you to work this out for the highest and greatest good for everyone concerned."

Then I "Let Go and Let God."

* * *

In less than three years' time I finished my schooling, had built up a somewhat steady stream of clients, and felt confident enough that I was able to fill that $300 a month gap to cover my health insurance.

In January of 2006, I made my retirement from the publishing house official. I could now totally devote myself to helping others in their healing.

At graduation, among my peers I was the only person who earned all three available certifications offered at the school at that time: Massage Therapist Practitioner, Wellness Consultant, and Energy Therapy Practitioner. And I was so proud of what I had accomplished that I stepped out of my comfort zone and asked if I could speak at the closing ceremony.

During the festivities, I shared with my fellow graduates why I'd wanted to become a massage therapist at my advanced age, and how I felt called to be able to, at times, provide low cost or free, quality, healing massage to people who might not be able to afford it.

Maya Angelou had said, "When we cast our bread upon the waters we can presume that someone downstream whose face we will never know will benefit from our action, as we who are downstream from another will profit from the grantor's gift."

That $2,000 annual tuition reimbursement from my job was a true gift, and it was an honor to be able to do the same for, like she said, "...someone downstream whose face we will never know [that] will benefit from our action..."

Many clients have come to me since then through referrals from a friend or relative happy with what I've been able to do for them. And it's always a pleasure to know that the energy behind what I'm doing is not just helping people physically, but mentally, emotionally, and spiritually as well.

Little did I know that channeling positive energy throughout the body would be exactly the thing that literally, saved my life.

Chapter 20
<u>Maybe Checking Out</u>
<u>Would be Better Than This</u>

I remember four very distinct times in my life when I seriously contemplated suicide.

The first was when I was about eight or nine years old after Pop and I had had one of our famous spats. He wanted me to work out in the shop, and I, of course, wanted to tend to things inside the house. You know, like baking sugar cookies and making pink lemonade!

Neither of us understood why the other didn't grasp their point. We just wanted things to go our way.

Later, still upset, I went out to the barn, found some twine we used for bailing hay, and bound it together to make it stronger. After trying to make it look like a noose based on what I remembered seeing on western shows on television, I stood on a bale of hay and threw it over one of the rafters. Just then, I heard mom calling the family in for dinner. So I went inside, forgetting all about my suicide preparations by the time we finished our meal.

Some 20 years later on a weekend visit back to see my parents, I went to the barn and the rope was still hanging there. "I was really going to do it," I thought.

That sad little boy now an older, wiser (and taller) man reached up, pulled it down, went in the house, hugged Eva and my adorable baby daughter, and thanked God I didn't go through with it.

* * *

The next time thoughts of suicide reared their ugly head we were living in Lincoln. And at that time no matter how you sliced it, my life—so I thought—was in the toilet.

As you may recall, I was in my 30s, my parents had passed within seven months of each other, and I was still feeling really cheated that they weren't around to watch Beth and David grow up. And my marriage was crazy and stressful as I continued to struggle with my sexuality, while also trying to hide my extramarital affairs from Eva.

Yes, I had started seeing Pastor Dennis and a therapist and things were getting better, but I was still carrying around the guilt of appearing to the outside world like a stand-up guy – an all-around "pillar of the community."

At work I felt like I just couldn't measure up to all the other guys who had office jobs, me being a lowly, somewhat introverted, blue collar printing pressman and all. And it didn't help that whenever the mood struck my boss would launch little jabs about my Baptist beliefs.

Taking a second job as a cab driver to help make ends meet only added to my shame, guilt, and feelings of low self-worth.

My relationship with booze became stronger (I started with vodka, hiding the bottles in my desk drawer files under "V" and later adding to the alphabet) and I upped the prescription drugs to deal with my emotional pain. This was well before the opioid crisis/prescription drug monitoring days, so I knew how to play physician roulette to get as many as I needed – some to slow me down; others to speed me up.

One day while sitting in my big living room chair, staring at the happy family portrait on top of the television I'd insisted we take (coincidentally, there were no happy faces in it) I thought, "What in the world? This thing (my sexuality) is not changing. I don't want to raise my kids with this around."

A few days later, at work there was a company blow up about something or other which emotionally pushed me to the limit.

That was it. It was time to check out.

So, I pulled out a sheet of paper and wrote a letter to Eva and the kids telling them how I wasn't worth anything and they'd be better off without me.

"At least they'd have a joyful holiday and the portrait (which I'd also made copies of for each of my siblings) to remember me by," I thought.

I put the letter in my desk drawer, choked down the remaining valium (also hiding in the "V" file), and left the office.

Somehow, I made it home, practically crawling up the steps and into the house. Eva was shocked at my appearance and kept asking me what was wrong. I just kept playing it off that I didn't feel well.

Thankfully, she and the kids went to church that night.

After more self-medicating from my home "pharmacy," I stumbled and fell and broke my glasses. I don't remember how I made it upstairs, but once there I took off my clothes, got into bed, pulled the covers up over my head, and slowly drifted off into what I hoped would be my last night on earth.

When I woke up the next morning, I realized I wasn't dead yet. This only magnified my shame and guilt.

I couldn't even die right.

* * *

I know the saying, *"Third time's a charm"* is supposed to be a good thing—a success of some kind—but my third attempt at taking my life was anything but charming.

It was during the time that Eva and I were in the process of divorce, I'd moved out of our home and was living in a one-bedroom apartment, my brother George was dying of cancer, and I and the folks at Broadway Church were still in the "fixing" stage of my being gay.

I was at an all-time low.

One night, while looking for love in all the wrong places to satisfy my urges and soothe my emotional pain, I went to a mall department store restroom where I'd gone many, many times before cruising for men. There I found a cute guy, suggestive signals were made back and forth, I asked for "a looksie," then learned he was an undercover vice cop.

I must have looked too defeated to even try to get out of it, or perhaps he sensed I wasn't a danger to anyone, because he took pity on me, saying he wouldn't use his handcuffs. However, he made it very clear that if he got even one inkling that I'd bolt, everyone in the mall would hear, see, and know I was getting arrested.

When we got to his squad car, he even put me in the front seat instead of the obvious jailbird spot in the back. I'm grateful that although he had a job to do, he was still willing to show me some compassion.

When released from the police station later that evening, I started the long, dark, chilly walk back the mall to get my car. At one point along the way, I looked up and saw a highway exit ramp.

"What if I just walk up there and get hit by a car and be done with it," I thought. But then I remembered the court papers in my pocket that I didn't want to be found on my dead body. So instead, I went to a service station and called one of the men in my support group. He came right away, we got my car from the mall, then went back to my apartment and talked for hours.

"John, on any given day, at any given moment, any human being can be their very best or their very worst," he told me. "This is not the worst thing you did; it just feels like it. But remember that this too shall pass."

Several weeks later, while waiting my turn to be called at the scheduled court appearance, I looked across the room and saw my nephew, Robert, my brother Foster's son, who was a Kansas City police officer. I was mortified that not only would someone I knew find out about my restroom incident, but it would be a relative!

Sweating bullets (no police officer pun intended!) that he might see me, I tried to make myself as small as possible in my seat for an agonizing 15 minutes. When my attorney and I finally stood before the judge, the charge of solicitation was reduced to disturbing the peace, I had to pay a fine, and was put on two years' probation. Hightailing it out the side door to avoid my nephew, I ran to the clerk's office to take care of the paperwork and get the hell out of there.

As luck would have it, while trying to make my hasty courthouse escape, I ran right into Robert. He started off by apologizing, saying he wasn't there to embarrass me, rather was in court (one he coincidentally is almost never in) for a case he was working on. Turns out he already knew about my arrest because the vice cop from the mall had put two-and-two together when he realized we both had the same unusual "Delameter" last name. Despite my public humiliation and shock at realizing a family member now knew about my dirty behavior, Robert, true to his nature, also showed me nothing but compassion.

Years later it occurred to me that what I was really running from was the one thing I badly needed and wanted – unconditional love.

Once home and back into my regular dreary life routine, I thought that only Eva and I (and now, of course, Robert) knew the real reason why we'd separated. She and I had agreed not to tell anyone, at least for now.

Turns out she had other plans.

Unbeknownst to me, she'd told just about everyone she knew about "my problem." She told my brothers and my sisters, and some of the people we worked with (when I confronted her about it later, she said she'd only told a few people and "they wouldn't tell anybody").

There were already rumors floating around about me at work that I was trying to ignore for as long as possible. But of course these types of things always spread as fast as butter on hot bread!

I was very angry and hurt that she'd gone behind my back and done this. I mean, it wasn't like she'd found out about my extramarital affairs by accident. She knew I'd been working on changing it; on trying to see if we could maybe get back together and put this whole era of our life behind us.

And she'd told the kids too, which was just devastating to me.

I found out when David called one day and said, "Mom told me about your little secret!" Beth was deeply hurt as well and had almost the same reaction.

David was still very angry and blaming me for our separation and the many changes that came with it: having to move from our lovely home into a small, two-bedroom apartment with his mom, Eva working two jobs to help make ends meet which also meant there was less money available for him to do or buy things ...

In retrospective, I suppose they may have both been grappling with thoughts like, "*Who is this person? How could this be true about my dad – the man who comforted me in the night during a storm when it went 'thunner' in my room? The one who helped me build race cars for my YMCA contests. The former deacon, and church bus driver, and husband. How could this be? And now he's gay?*"

It was a very rough and challenging time for all of us.

Even though I tried my best to explain myself to them, it was all in vain.

Most people in Eva's and my social circles were understanding, or at least they tried to be. But there was backlash from some of the Delameter siblings. And rightfully so. They'd just learned something new about their brother, and pretty much all they knew about being gay were the stereotypes they'd seen on TV and the like.

Most of them said nothing to me about it, and two or three were very encouraging. So, I least I had a nice mixed "bouquet of flowers" to work with.

When I shared all of this with my therapist he said, "John, you've known all your life that you preferred men, but this was new information for them. Of course, they're having a hard time trying to understand."

But the end result was the same. My life-long secret was out—really out—to everyone who knew me. It took me right back to when I was called a "Sissy" and a "Momma's Boy" when I was little, reigniting the hurt, embarrassment, shame, and guilt around that.

Everyone now knew, I couldn't control it, and I had no idea what to do about it.

My pile of shame was growing taller, larger, heavier, and more unbearable by the day. It was only a matter of time before the big fat disgraceful bubble that was my life would burst.

At one of my counseling appointments following all of this I told the therapist, "I want you to know that you've saved my life many times. You've walked beside me through a lot of pain. But this is not working. So, if my kids ever came to you with questions about anything we've discussed, you have my full permission to share the details of our conversations." And along with that, I kept dropping subtle hints about taking my life.

Not falling for it, he called me out, saying he wouldn't be part of any kind of suicide threats.

Instead, to help me gain a little perspective he handed me a list of positive affirmations written by author and motivational speaker Zig Ziglar. Then he made me stand and read them aloud.

Among them were:

Always remember that your present situation is not your final destination. The best is yet to come.

Sometimes adversity is what you need to face in order to become successful.

Your attitude, not your aptitude, will determine your altitude.

Of course I didn't want to hear any of this positive stuff, preferring to wallow in my own misery and self-pity. But he made me read them anyway and when I got to the end of the list, I did feel a little bit better.

Until I got home.

My apartment was an absolute wreck. There were clothes draped on furniture and all over the floor, empty, stale food containers and dirty dishes were strewn about, there were piles of unopened mail, and a lot of stuff obviously just landed wherever I'd thrown it.

This outer chaos was a direct reflection of what I felt about myself on the inside: I was a complete and total disaster. I had "tried everything" but none of it was going my way. Sure, I saw a few glimpses of hope in what I'd read, but in my mind, I just knew that it wouldn't last.

So I immediately threw the affirmation paper away, swallowed the last of my sleeping pills, drained a bottle of booze, crawled into bed, and hoped that *finally* this would be the end. It may sound cliché, but it was definitely my "Dark Night of the Soul."

Goodbye world. I'm sorry, but I tried my best. You'll all be better off without me.

Waking up in the middle of the night sick from the substances I'd tossed down my throat, I crawled out of what I'd hoped was my deathbed and went in search of those crumpled up Zig Ziglar affirmations. It's a wonder I could even find them, given the state of my completely disheveled apartment.

Barely able to stand, my body swaying all over the place, I read them aloud, again … and again … and again. They just lifted me above the low self-worth stories I had been telling myself and provided a little light in my dark tunnel.

When I look back at all of these suicide attempts, I realize that every time, something came along to stop it:

My mother calling the family in for dinner.

Waking up after taking what I'd hoped would snuff me out for good.

The court papers in my pocket I didn't want to be found on my dead body if I'd been killed walking up that highway exit ramp.

The Zig Ziglar quotes from my therapist.

Perhaps it was God, or angels, or some other life force watching over me. Whatever it was, it always kept me from going through with it.

I was slowly beginning to feel like maybe there just might be something in my life that was going to work after all.

Chapter 21
<u>So, Now What?</u>

Now that the divorce from Eva was final and she had moved on, I could officially start dating. Still kind of thinking I could be straight, I decided to "test things out" by seeking out the company of women and doing the usual things like going out to eat, dancing, and to the movies. And hopefully, like "Sheldon Cooper" from the TV show *The Big Bang Theory* would say, have a little coitus too!

Once I started having sex with other women, I came to the conclusion that I was simply attracted to men. If 31 years of marriage didn't change me, what would?

So, it was back to dating men.

Even though my therapist and I had agreed after the vagina-in-the-hot-tub incident for me to spend about a year in a healthy gay lifestyle without trying to fix it, I was cautious.

That meant there was no "touchy feely" stuff at all in public.

If at the movies or the theater, we waited until after the lights went down to hold hands.

In a restaurant I was very careful where we sat. But after a while I preferred to dine in predominantly gay restaurants where you could cuddle and hold hands, and nobody would bat an eye.

At a baseball game, if attendance was a little sparsely populated in our section, regardless of our assigned seats I'd be sure the two of us moved closer to other people so we wouldn't stand out. But I hadn't really thought that one out very clearly because, *HELLO*, guys go to sporting events together all the time and no one ever thinks anything of it. But when you're trying to hide your sexuality you sometimes take "being undercover" too far!

When talking about my dating life, I always made it a point to refer to "she" – "she" fixed this for dinner, "she" said this, and so forth to make sure people wouldn't find out I was really with a man.

Although Eva had already spilled the beans about me at work, I was still terrified that one of my co-workers might see me going in or out of a gay bar on a Saturday night. So I'd park far away from the building to a spot where I could hide in the shadows and monitor who else was coming and going before I made my move. To somewhat ease my mind, I joked that I'd probably be fine because most of them would already be home in bed by 10 p.m. due to early Sunday School the next morning!

I did have one close friend at work who was straight, and we'd shared a lot of things over the years (including all my lies about the women I was dating and what I liked about them). Eventually, I trusted him enough to fully fess up.

"If you have any questions, don't hesitate to ask," I said.

"Well, I'd heard some rumor about that a few months ago, but you didn't say anything so I just kind of let it go," he responded.

Nevertheless, he appreciated the gesture and said he felt honored that I would trust him with my Truth.

About 30 minutes later he came back over to my work area and said, "I do have one question: Are you a 'poker' or a 'pokee'?" We both got a good laugh out of that one!

It wasn't too long, however, before some of my greatest fears started appearing in real time.

During trips to the men's room I'd hear things like, "I get nervous when you come in here."

On another occasion, I was in the lunchroom when a guy from another department came in wearing the same shirt. I didn't hear exactly what was whispered among the guys on the other side of the room, but it was along the lines of he and I "liking the same things."

And a carpool buddy suddenly decided that "his schedule changed" and he wasn't going to be able to exchange rides anymore. Strangely enough, every night after that at the same time I was standing at the bus stop, he'd drive by. Each time I just waved.

Somehow, by the grace of God, I kept my job.

I was trying to handle it all the best that I could, but the stress was taking its toll.

At one of my next therapy visits I shared how I always looked forward to weekends off, but after church on Sunday I'd become depressed and upset.

My therapist's response was, "That's because on Monday morning you have to be someone that you're not."

That helped me better understand that all these years I'd been living as the person I wasn't.

On the family front, things weren't that much better.

Because everyone was still trying to figure out how to navigate these new unchartered waters, things were a bit strained.

Beth and David, though they struggled, were the first to really come around to embracing me for who I was. My son-in-law, Brian, remained cordial but our relationship definitely changed.   But over the years we've been able to work through our issues as well, and have built a real honest, strong relationship.

If you took a poll among my siblings, asking their opinion of me post-coming out (well, really post-being outed) on a scale of 1 to 10: 1 being that I'm going to hell, and 10 being "What's the big deal?" overall the family was at about a 6.

Some said it was a sin. Others asked, "How could you just ruin your life like that?" And there was lots of guilt heaped on me about "poor little Eva" giving me the best years of her life. Well, I had also given the best years of my life; a life I was always trying to "fix" for her and our family.

Then there were those dumping guilt on me with, "After all that Mother and Daddy did for you, you go and throw your life away like this!"

It's no wonder I stopped going to family reunions for a few years. I just didn't want to hear or deal with any of it. Dealing with it myself was hard enough without the extra burden of the disgrace some were trying to force upon me.

Looking back at that time now, I can clearly see and understand how this Southern Baptist family had been completely broadsided with something they never expected. So of course it was only natural that they didn't know what to do with this new revelation. Our family was born and raised in the 1920s, '30s and '40s, well before it was acceptable to speak openly about one's sexuality - whether about a man or a woman.

I, on the other hand, had had years of trying to come to terms with it.

It really helped when a friend told me that their new knowledge was just an add-on to what they already knew about me. All I had to do, he said, was just continue living my life and things would eventually work themselves out. They were just doing the best they could. In other words, like I'd been told before, "This too shall pass."

Over time the tides have changed, and they've all come to accept that inside—in my heart—I'm still the same person they've always known and loved.

An example of this, in addition to the note I previously received from a niece, was a heartfelt letter from my now late sister, Lillian. She acknowledged the fact that although we were poles apart in our spiritual beliefs, she did love and accept me, even if she didn't agree with "what I was doing." She missed seeing me at the family reunions and hoped I'd come again soon.

I wrote her back, saying I would at some point. But only if she understood that I wasn't going to try to change her, and that she wouldn't try to change me. She agreed, adding, "We will do what Mother and Daddy would have wanted us to do: make-up, get along, and just love each other."

Fast forward to today and only five Delameter siblings remain: Me, Lea, Derald, Twylia, and Jo, and we're as close as ever. And in the years since I've come out, I've experienced nothing but love and acceptance from them and their families.

We all grow up in families with different beliefs, customs, lifestyles, and opinions about what's "right and wrong." But as we grow older and get out on our own, we form our own opinions and make our own decisions. Sometimes they line up with those from our family of origin, and sometimes they don't.

But at the end of the day, I believe that even though we may not understand or approve of what's going on, we should still accept and love each other.

To me, that's the real definition of a family.

Chapter 22
<u>Not Just Pretty Boys Making Pretty Music</u>

In every church I've ever attended—as a boy in Princeton, at our family churches in Lincoln and Dahlonega, and at both Broadway and MCC—I've sung in the choir.

I always loved seeing a group of people come together with the common goal of producing good music. Sometimes there were difficulties trying to match the parts during rehearsals, but once the performance night came it all worked. It still gives me chills to hear each part of a chorus break out into their particular harmonies, and feedback from the audience about how they connected with us and were moved across a range of emotions.

Through music, we can heal.

At one point, someone told me about the Heartland Men's Chorus (HMC). It started in 1986 as a small group of men wanting to form a choral group and has continued to grow ever since, becoming the largest and highest profile gay organization in the Kansas City region.

For some time I'd thought about auditioning for them, but I was afraid to do it while still working at the publishing house given the overall company religious beliefs about homosexuality being a sin.

One of the things that drew me to the HMC was their mission to use their voices to "enlighten, inspire, heal and empower," which I really felt they did in every production. But they didn't just sing. Every performance was a complete entertainment experience, like a Broadway show. They combined many different music styles, choreography, special sets and lighting, themed costumes, and other production elements. And behind all of it, the messages were always about acceptance, celebrating diversity, and creating change in the world.

At one particular Christmas concert there was an audience sing-along portion, and I was just belting it out! Later, at intermission, a lady sitting next to me said she was so impressed with my voice, she thought I should be up there singing too!

I always remembered that, so after I retired, I auditioned and they said, "Yes!" Soon I'd be singing, not in the audience, but onstage before hundreds of people.

Like my experiences at Broadway and MCC, the HMC members came from different ethnic, cultural, socio-economic, and religious backgrounds. They were fathers, sons, and uncles, and really no different than someone's neighbor, or a restaurant employee, or cashier at the grocery store. And there were straight people and women in the chorus as well. It was all so inclusive.

My bass voice fit right in, and I was so proud to join these wonderful people who were out and felt so free to be themselves. They all just enjoyed good music and really cared about singing out healing for other men, women, and young people.

There were many songs in the productions that really spoke to me, going right to my core. For example, the lyrics in "They Sang to Me" talked about being alone in the dark among the crowd wondering about your life, afraid to be seen or to come out.

But then you see and hear these brave men and women whose united voices seem to be singing directly to you – to your heart. They seem to know and understand your innermost thoughts while singing about hope, love, life, and pride.

That had been me over the years. I'd wanted to feel that sense of freedom, pride, and joy for so long, and now I had it.

The memory of that night still brings tears to my eyes because I know there are others—maybe even young boys or girls—who will hear us and feel in their hearts, "They sang to me."

Stephen Sondheim's "Not While I'm Around" from the play *Sweeney Todd*—about standing up for someone in the face of potential harm—was another one that brought me great joy. In "When I Knew," we used chorus and family member voice recordings as part of the production to share what it felt like to realize that you, or someone you loved, was gay.

Revealing what bullying can look like in adults to the bus loads of kids who came for a matinee performance of "Oliver Button is a Sissy" was another of my favorites.

My most impactful moment, I think, was when some of us brought our childhood photos and gave testimonials about our suicide attempts as part of the global "It Gets Better Project" supporting LGBTQ+ youth. What I want people, especially today's young people, to know is that when things are so messed up, and so dark, and you think suicide is the answer, it's not. Just hang in there because it *does* get better.

Not too long ago there was a Honda Civic commercial showing a guy named Mark. And while Mark is walking out of a warehouse toward the street, the camera switches between his wife, a co-worker, and a close friend saying great things about him. And just as he steps out a car is approaching, and you hear the brakes screech.

The next scenes are of those same people, except they are in agony. His wife, who is holding their newborn son, and his co-worker, are crying, and his close friend is standing there in shock.

Luckily, Mark wasn't hit by the car because it was equipped with a special sensing system that alerted the driver that someone was in front of him, and he had enough time to apply the brakes.
The last scene is of Mark going home to his loving family, with these words appearing across the screen:

Collisions affect more than those involved.

The last part of that commercial is what I really want people to realize:

If you give up and give in to the darkness and take your life, there are many things your friends and family who love you will miss out on. And you will miss out on them too.

Had I been successful in any of my suicide attempts, I wouldn't have been able to see my kids grow up, attend their graduations and weddings, experience the joys of grandparenting, or get to sing on stage with this amazing chorus. Leaving this earth like that would have been a real tragedy and a loss for everybody.

Giving in to the darkness is not the answer.

Now as you've probably guessed by now, this far into my book, I do have a little flair for the dramatic at times! So of course I absolutely loved the time when the chorus sang Lady Gaga's "Born This Way."

While dancing under the rainbow flag-colored strobe lights we did kind of a Chippendale's thing, whipping off our fancy tuxedo jackets to reveal the printed t-shirts we were wearing underneath: "SISSY." "LIKES GUYS." "GEEK." And on some of the straight guys in the group, "LIKES GALS." It was a riot and really brought the house down!

After the Stage 4 cancer diagnosis I was in another production where the last song we sang was, "You Will Never Walk Alone."

It's all about continuing to move forward, even when the storms of life cast a shadow over our path. To push back our fears and not succumb to the darkness, but instead hold our heads up high, look towards the light, and know that there are others supporting and walking beside us - always.

No matter what, we will never walk alone

I'd heard this song all my life, but it didn't speak to me as deeply as it did that night.

Right up until that point, I'd been thinking that the cancer had me and I'd never be on this stage again.

Yet I knew that as things progressed, my chorus family would be there to support me and my family in our time of need.

Chapter 23
Out of the Closet

As children, maybe just to survive in our family of origin, we do whatever we have to do to fit in. But as we grow older, simply going through the motions and accepting things as "just the way they are," is not authentic living.

The "real deal" is intimacy, vulnerability, and a willingness to engage in dialogue with people about what you truly believe, as well as acknowledging—with others and within yourself—anything that no longer resonates with what you may have been told. What you are or are not. How you need to dress, or behave, or worship. Who to love or reject. The totality of what your life is "supposed" to look like.

I didn't know why at the time but ever since I was a little boy, I've always searched for answers to improve my life and just assumed everybody else sought self-improvement too. But as an adult I realized there are those who have chosen to be comfortable with the way things have always been.

From way back in elementary school I remember a ledge where we stacked our boots. It became the place where kids would sit and tell me all of their problems. For some reason they seemed to be very comfortable with me, and I apparently had a knack for compassionate solutions.

Another memory from that time was a weekly reader the school subscribed to filled with current events and a lot of other articles for kids. This included a column where they could submit questions about problems they were having. Using my "gift," I'd read and answer them to myself first, then see how the editors responded (Decades later at my 50th high school reunion, one of my classmates asked if I remembered sitting on that ledge with him all those years ago listening to his problems!).

And then there was the 1950s television show "For Better or Worse" that featured real life couples dealing with real life issues. It wasn't something that our family made it a point to watch, but the TV was usually on when the show started at noon which was right around the same time we gathered on non-school days for lunch. Once again, I was captivated when listening to their personal stories and trying to decide what advice I'd give them, just like the host therapist on the show.

When I got to high school, there was a subscription to the *St. Joseph Gazette* newspaper which included the "Ask Ann Landers" column. There, too, I would read about people's issues, personally answer them, then read her responses to see how my advice lined up. My childhood "career path" must have been developing really well because Ann and I often had some of the same responses.

So I guess emotional and personal growth has always been a way of life for me.

Unlike those submitting their problems in print however, my parents would've had no one to talk to if they had even the faintest idea that I was gay, except maybe our Baptist preacher. But I have doubts about that.

Mother was always insistent that all of us look good in front of him —from our clothes, to our behavior, to the things we said. To this day I still remember her saying things like, "What would Brother Harry say about that?" Or "What would Brother Harry say if he knew you did that?" And "What would Brother Harry say if he knew you were like that?"

Going to Brother Harry, whether it was her or me, to talk about thoughts of being gay would have probably never happened.

When I finally and fully embraced my homosexuality, I still had a great deal of self-talk to work through just to refer to myself as a gay man. That required dismantling decades of hiding it, and denying the conversations echoing in my head—with myself and others—that said it was "not OK." This included tons of old biblical stories about going to hell and living in damnation forever.

Over the years, what I've learned about myself and others is that change can be very difficult. We stay stuck in bad relationships, or jobs, or addictive behaviors because even though we know it's not good for us, we also know what to expect. If we choose to step out of the thing that's not working, we have no idea what our life might look like. And that can feel scarier than where we are now.

But once I made the decision to embrace the perfect expression of God I was born to be, I knew it was my choice what I wanted to do and how I wanted to live. I decided to name it and claim it. Being gay wasn't the "all of me" but it was a part of me.

The closet had been opened and for the first time in my life— at age 60—I was experiencing a great deal of freedom. That's what part of this healing journey has been about. The interpretation of my life and experiences had changed to what I—not the church, nor my family, nor anyone else—believed.

I often joke that the only way I would ever go back in the closet is if I could decorate it first! And take someone nice in there with me!

But in all seriousness, I had found the truth: *I was born this way. And I'd been set free.*

* * *

Despite my new sense of personal freedom and the rumors swirling around because Eva had started spilling the beans, I still wasn't ready to officially "come out" at work. I had only a few years to go until retirement and didn't want to get mysteriously fired and have to find another job.

Although the company had always been so good to Eva and I over the years, even after we separated and divorced, and they were such good people, and I truly loved my job, I just didn't agree with a lot of their cultural rules and politics.

For one, women could wear earrings, but they couldn't be flashy or dangling. The men, on the other hand, were prohibited from wearing any at all.

There were also very tight guidelines—both stated and implied—about how we dressed. What even today might be considered the most modest V-Neck blouse on a woman would have raised some eyebrows. Appearing like we could've been on our way to church was the expected norm.

The first time I heard some guy say something about sex in passing while in the office, I turned to him and said, "I've been here about a month and no one has cracked one joke about sex. I was beginning to think maybe I was the only person here who knew anything about that!"

It was all just part of the religious culture there.

So I resolved that, again, if talking about a date, or personal relationship, or anything along those lines, to keep on referring to the person I was talking about as "she." But only until I received my last paycheck!

As my retirement date got closer, I could feel the ties that bound me loosening. And at my going away celebration I decided to cut the cord and officially set myself free by boldly telling people that I had auditioned and been accepted to sing in a production with the HMC.

On my last day of work, I clocked out at 3:30 p.m., and about an hour later I had a brand-new earring in my left ear (in the gay world, left is "right," and right is "wrong!"). That was the last hold on my balls! For me, it was a symbol that I was now as free as I wanted to be. I could go anywhere I wanted, do anything, and express myself in any way I desired and deserved.

In the years thereafter when I stopped by to visit (wearing my earring, of course!), I felt no shame in responding to their questions about what I was doing these days, whether it was singing with the HMC, participating in a dinner theater production at MCC, giving massages, attending the annual Gay Pride Parade...there was no longer anything to hide.

It felt so good to be me—John—not "Gay John," living my life. And you know what? Most of my former coworkers still accepted me for me.

Just as I would learn later during the cancer scare, when I believe what I know versus what I am told, life begins to change.

I was out of the closet, and I was free.

Chapter 24
<u>But We also Know Something</u>

My divorce was final, I had retired, I was fully out as a gay man, I was still attending MCC, and there had been a five-year gap since my first few visits with Richard.

Sometimes when we hear something new that we don't understand, we reject it. But once time goes by and we grow—intellectually, spiritually, or otherwise—we realize that the strange information we'd heard before may have something in it for us after all.

The last time I saw Richard I wasn't ready to explore spiritual and intuitive ways to address the various issues in my life. And although I was now eager to jump in with both feet, there were so many things going on with me that I didn't know where to start first.

Despite coming out, my low self-esteem and "I'm not good enough" stories were still very present. And because of this, I always kept my guard up around other people.

An unhealthy relationship with food and being overweight were two other issues. These went all the way back to when my younger brother Jerrie and I were growing up.

I don't know why, but my mother always dressed us alike. And because we were less than a year apart in age, people would ask if we were twins. Jerrie was "the skinny one," and I was "the fat one."

And when we wore the blue Montgomery Ward swimsuits mother bought us, folks said we looked like those diet pill ads. I was the "Before" (overweight), and Jerrie was the "After" (when the extra weight was gone).

And let's not forget about the out-of-town relative (who shall remain nameless), who every time she came to visit would say to me, "Oh Johnnie, you're just getting so fat! Fat, fat, river rat!" It's no wonder I had such low self-esteem around my size.

I felt some relief from all of that when Jerrie got his tonsils out, because I believed the wives' tale that said you gain weight when this happens.

"Now Jerrie will get fat like me too," I said to myself.

But the kicker is, neither of us was really skinny nor fat. But those hurtful words from others really stung, becoming part of the negative self-talk I'd told myself for decades.

Sticks and stones may break your bones, but names can beat the life out of you.

Years later I was sharing my childhood weight stories with my therapist, who had a really fun sense of humor. It may not have been professional, but he sure did make me laugh when he said it was OK for me to let go of those old hurtful words from my—and he couldn't remember her name—so he said, "Aunt Bitch!" That was hilarious and still makes me laugh!

Once Richard and I started digging into my upbringing, we realized my inability to be intimate with someone, and not necessarily always in a sexual nature, probably went back to being molested by a male relative as a child. Even though it only happened once, it was so traumatic that I didn't even realize my adolescent mind had buried it so deeply. And there are parts about it that I still don't remember, even to this day.

Shutting down to avoid reliving the physical and emotional pain, I learned, definitely affected not only my relationships but knowing how to treat myself with love and compassion.

The unfortunate thing is that when we shut down to keep out the bad stuff, we also close the door on how to allow good feelings to come in. As a result, we restrict our ability to form healthy relationships with other people.

Our work together was slow but steady, and after two- or three-years' time Richard and I had built up a lot of trust and mutual respect. I guess you could say that when the student is ready, the teacher is eager to expand their consciousness too!

It also helped that Richard was an avid book collector (he has over 3,000 in his home), and he always had lots of inspiring quotes from a wide variety of religious and spiritual scholars and teachers to share with me.

Richard was (and still is) very pleased that I was so open to learning. And he really committed himself to helping me discover and expand my awareness of the beauty and light within me. I was like a sponge soaking up all of this new information and insights, and I just couldn't get enough of it.

One of the most significant things Richard taught me was about the work of a chiropractor by the name of Dr. George Goodheart.

Over 55 years ago, Dr. Goodheart began bridging the gap between kinesiology or "Muscle Testing"—the study and care of our musculature system—and our thinking and emotions. What he found is that by using the body as a diagnostic tool, it was possible to dramatically increase a person's overall health and well-being. The way to accomplish this was by tapping into the subconscious mind through the energy field found in the muscles and organs of the body - the places where we store everything that has happened and is currently happening in our lives.

Richard was also familiar with the work of Dr. Bradley Nelson, a very well-known and respected holistic physician and lecturer who wrote the book, *The Emotion Code*. His book also focused on how to tap into and release the emotionally charged events that inhabit our body to support overall wellness.

Between these and other resources, Richard really understood how our emotions can get in the way, preventing us from having a full-healing process.

"We all sometimes get these emotional blocks around what we make up in our heads about what's going on in our lives, or by not being true to who we are," Richard explained. "And over time our body starts talking to us through things that show up as pain, or illnesses, or diseases. But the body has a way to heal, and it *knows* how to heal itself. All we need to do is speak to it *directly.*"

To start the process, Richard would take his client's hand and invite the spiritual masters or guides from the past or present to arrive for healing. And while doing so, if any other, what some might call "evil spirits" arrived, he would ask them to leave.

Richard would then consult the Emotion Code chart created by Dr. Nelson. On it, different parts of the body are grouped together and listed in a vertical column on the left-hand side, and the emotions associated with them are in two other vertical columns to the right.

For example, Row 1 represents the Heart or Small Intestine, which are listed in the top, left column. Row 1, Column A (in the middle) states the emotions of Abandonment, Betrayal, Forlorn, Lost, and Love Unreceived. Row 1, Column B (on the right) reflects Effort Unreceived, Heartache, Insecurity, Overjoy, and Vulnerability.

Row 4 represents the Liver or Gall Bladder, with Column A reflecting Anger, Bitterness, Guilt, Hatred, and Resentment, and Column B reflecting Depression, Frustration, Indecisiveness, Panic, and Taken for Granted.

Using the chart, Richard would speak to his client's body in the form of a statement.

Remember Richard's decades-earlier Irritable Bowel Syndrome problem? He'd had the same type of "conversation" with the Native American healer who stated that he could digest milk products, and just allowed his body to answer truthfully. For him, the answer was no, he could not digest milk products.

With the Emotion Code chart, responses can be even more specifically identified in the body.

So again, imagine that you're standing up with your right arm extended horizontally from your body. Richard would then put a little pressure on your wrist or arm with his hand, as if trying to push it down, and say, for example, "There is a problem, an emotional blockage, in Row 1 (Heart or Small Intestine)."

If he was *unable* to push your wrist or arm down, then the statement was false: you were not experiencing any issues with the emotions in Column A or B. But if he *was* able to move it—the hand or wrist often falling straight down to the side without much resistance at all—then there was something further to explore.

"This process is a trusting of my intuition to what I am feeling in the client, and it took me almost a year-and-a-half to trust this," Richard explained.

In this example, what he'd sometimes find was an overall issue with walling off the heart at some point in the client's life as a defense mechanism, which has since prevented them from expressing vulnerability or forming intimate relationships. With me, he'd hit the nail right on the head; everything that I'd stuffed down since childhood—the molestation, confusion around my sexuality, feeling inferior to everyone else, and so on—all played a role in my inability to be completely open and vulnerable with others.

Just being able to identify this was an eye-opener, and in that instant, I felt like my walls were beginning to crumble.

* * *

"You need to know before I get there for my next appointment what's going on," I told Richard when he answered the phone.

It was only about a week down the road from the life-altering call from the oncologist, and I didn't want to blindside him in person.

He, like my friend Bill, the first person I'd told about my diagnosis, was speechless for a bit. But even over the phone I felt like his heart was going out to me.

When I arrived at his office for my next appointment, I had this kind of hopeless feeling surrounding me. I could still hear the glass marbles cascading down the stairs at warp speed, and it seemed like there was nothing I could do to stop them.

I started by filling him in on the specifics of my diagnosis:

Most of the cancer had been found in my liver and lymph nodes and would probably spread to other parts of my body.

There was a fairly new type of chemotherapy we could try, and with it I could possibly live a couple of months longer than the six-to-eight months he had predicted.

Despite any measures, I was still going to die.

"But I don't want to do that," I told Richard. "Even though chemo and radiation are supposed to help you in the long run, I know how destructive they are to the body. If the doctor is right, and I'm going to die soon, I don't want my last few months to be in worse condition than I am right now."

Richard explained that Western medicine as we know it today is allopathic—traditional, science-based, and primarily using medication or surgery to resolve any issues. "But that's just one opinion," he said. "There's also you, using your own body and your own mental outlook, to heal. You can call it spiritual healing, mental healing, or emotional healing. But it is a healing."

In addition to using the Emotion Code chart, some therapists and energy healers also use a special kinesiology magnet to activate the energy running up and down your spine. Some look like black or silver hockey pucks with a big hole in the middle, but they are a lot thinner and about the same size or a little larger than a 50-cent coin.

Richard's magnet reminded me of a little gold-colored Chess pawn, and he kept it in a beautiful wooden box.

And again, almost like a direct telephone line connection to the subconscious mind, it reacts when your body is presented with certain statements, revealing any organs that may be weakened.

"That's the beauty of muscle testing," Richard said. "We just need to ask the body what's best for us, and it will answer. The body does not lie. It cannot lie."

A few weeks later, after repeating my objection to the doctor's suggestion, Richard said that if I wanted to, we could try using the magnet and Emotion Code chart. It is definitely not an easy concept for everyone to grasp at first, he said, and there needs to be a readiness to enter into that kind of thinking. But by then I had learned enough through my massage energy work to know that I was ready and willing to open myself up even further.

"I never make any promises, nor would I ever tell anybody not to see their doctors," said Richard. "And I'm never going to tell you what NOT to do. But you don't have to accept this condition as a death sentence. You can be the exception."

At that point Richard was the *only* person giving me any hope. It was my choice to believe what I wanted to believe about my healing, so I thought, *What do I have to lose?"*

Suddenly, it felt like somebody actually had something that just might help me.   And no matter what happened, he'd walk beside me every step of the way.

I'm fortunate that despite the cancer invading my liver and lymph nodes I had no pain, so relief drugs weren't necessary. For right now, Richard, the magnet energy work, Emotion Code chart, and prayer were all the prescriptions I needed.

Our work together was enlightening. On any particular visit, if I experienced a reaction from one of the statements Richard posed to my body, he might say, for example, "There's something going on in Row 5 (Kidneys or Bladder). Would you like to talk about that?"

And every time I'd say, "yes," many times also realizing that the emotions associated with that particular row had been coming up for me in recent days.

Turning to the magnet again and running it down my back, Richard would then encourage me to re-language my thoughts from, for example, "I am fearful" to "I feel the *presence* of fear, and "I'm ready and willing to totally, freely, and completely let that go, right here and right now."

After saying this three times, he'd check me again to see if I had truly let the negative emotions go.

I often noticed that once I said I was willing to let go of a particular thing, I'd belch and get a strange metallic taste in my mouth. That, I learned, was my body again speaking to me, trying to purge any negative emotions or energy that may have been holding the cancer in place.

"I'm not a medical doctor, so I don't want to make false statements. However, I do know that in a normal person with everything functioning well, troublesome cells are isolated and destroyed by the body system," he explained. "But we also all have the potential for cells in our body to go malignant very easily, and the body doesn't know what to do with that if it's being held back by a belief system or something that happened in our lives somewhere along the way. Once we acknowledge those blocks, then the whole system kicks in, finds any issues, and does what a healthy body does. So the potential is there for all of us to maintain good health."

After doing this for a few weeks, I remember driving home one day thinking, "This just might work."

About six weeks later, after repeat scans of my liver and lymph nodes, the customary blood work re-checks and all, I was sitting in the hallway waiting for my oncologist to give me the latest update (Quick funny story: somewhere along the way a friend pointed out that for some reason I kept saying I was there to see the "gynecologist," not the "oncologist." So I learned the difference between two big words!)

Unlike our previous appointments, I noticed a twinkle in his eye and a lightness in his steps along the cold, sterile, hospital floor.

The tumors had shrunk a little bit.

"But these things will do this," he said. In typical doctor-lingo he explained that I still had cancer but, "We'll keep an eye on it." In other words, *Things look good, but beware.*

A few weeks later, the tumors had shrunk even further.

I was ecstatic, joyful, and hopeful! The energy work Richard and I had been doing was paying off, and for the first time since the devastating diagnosis I was actually gaining hope for a positive future.

Oh my God! This is really happening! I thought.

It's important to note, however, that although I didn't want to keep hearing the doctor's somber warnings, I was still in a place where I felt I needed a medical opinion. And to his credit, despite the words of warning, I received nothing but love, support, and respect from him and his staff.

These two forms of input were polar opposite approaches—or choices—I guess I could say, of what I chose to believe. Between the medical professionals and Richard, I had the best of both worlds. For now, listening to both messages would have to do.

Three or so monthly check-up appointments later, however, it was a completely different story.

"The tumors have shrunk *again*. What are you doing?" my oncologist asked me, astonished.

So, I explained it: My work with Richard, the Emotion Code chart, using the magnet, and how I was holding thoughts of health and wholeness; sending ripples of light and healing to every cell of my body in my daily prayer and meditation time (and when no one was looking, I hugged a tree or two!). I was choosing to raise my vibration and focus my thoughts on life, not death.

"Well, I have known other people to do things similar to this," he responded. "So whatever is working for you, do it. But understand again, that this is serious. I am a man of science, and this is what we know about it."

I completely understood. Nevertheless, Richard's words kept coming back to me:

"But we also know something."

Chapter 25
Getting Ready for the End

The clock was ticking.

Time was of the essence.

Despite my incredible progress with my health and my work with Richard, I was still living in "the human world" and needed to start getting ready for the end.

Most of my pain at this point was emotional, but there were some physical symptoms as well: jaundice, an upset stomach, diarrhea, and a constant feeling of being wrung out and run down.

Oh! That was ME the doctor had called with the horrible news thought was another mental burden from time to time.

At this point, other than my doctor, my friend Bill, Richard, and my family, I'd told no one about my diagnosis and impending death.

That was about to change.

A mid-week service at MCC had just finished and I was walking out of the back door, through the beautiful reflection garden, then toward the security gates and parking lot beyond. As I passed through, Pastor Kurt, who had always been so loving and supportive of me, was about to lock the gates for the night. When he saw me, he asked how I was doing and I decided that now would be a good time to fill him in.

While filling him in on everything that had been going on, I got a little emotional and tears started welling up in my eyes. Already leaning on the bars of the gates to steady myself, he instinctively reached through and we held each other's hands. He would keep praying for me, he said, and if I or my family needed anything, he was here for us and I could call on him anytime.

In between all of these doctor appointments, on Easter morning when I went outside, I looked at my garden and there stood one bright, beautiful daffodil in the midst of the rest of the bulbs that were still dormant. For those of you who may not know, daffodils are among the first flowers to bloom in Spring and have been adopted as an international symbol of hope in the fight against cancer.

I took that brilliant spot of color as a message from God to not give up, that everything was OK, and He was still with me.

A few days before I was getting ready to start sharing what was happening with other people, I sent a Facebook message to my daughter filled with details about the latest appointments with my doctor. Well, I thought I was writing a private message to her, but accidentally posted it on my wall! Needless to say, the bad news spread like wildfire.

It's so interesting, yet understandable, how people don't know what to say when they hear about something like this. Some will talk to you, but talk *around* the subject, I'm guessing because they don't want to upset you, or make you feel bad if you're having a good day.

I soon learned to start with, "I'm sure you heard about my diagnosis…" and they would inevitably say, "Yes, and I'm so sorry," and then we could talk about it.

At one point, Pastor Kurt and I thought it would be a good idea for Beth and David to meet him, so they had some familiarity with each other before my health got much worse. When our group discussion got to the "what kind of final arrangements do you want" part, the kids said, "Whatever you want, Daddy."

We cried a lot that day.

Not long afterwards, I began thinking about how the kids didn't really know any of my friends. I wanted them to have a least some kind of connection with others who meant so much to me when the time came, so I invited them to our MCC senior's group, followed by lunch with a few of the members. I also made arrangements for other similar group get-togethers, which went well. They were very comfortable with doing this and enjoyed meeting my friends, and that helped put my mind at ease.

For my actual funeral I didn't want a somber, holier than thou type of thing where people would walk out thinking, "Who were they talking about in there?" I wanted it to be realistic and truthful about my life and my struggles.

The kids and I agreed that because of my love of gardening the service should have a botanical theme, including a slideshow of the different beautiful gardens I'd planted over the years. They even wanted to bring some of my old gardening clothes and flip-flops, but I had already secretly planned to throw those out before I made my grand exit!

For my cremated remains I bought a brand-new terracotta pot. I wanted an open vessel buried under the soil so when it rained the water would spread me into the earth.

Ashes to ashes, dust to dust.

Of course the gang from the HMC had to come to sing some of my favorite songs. "Great is Thy Faithfulness."

Other possible parts of my service discussed were Beth and David presenting a special reading, my granddaughter, Mikey, who was in high school at the time and a wonderful dancer, performing an interpretive dance with one of the guys from the church, and the other grandchildren sharing special memories they had with me, if any one of them felt comfortable doing so.

And I wanted the men who put on the first Sunday of the month potluck to fix their famous baked fried chicken for lunch and, like always, everyone else would bring the side dishes! During the meal there would be an open mic for those who wanted to share anything as well.

About a week later I drove to Chillicothe to meet my sister, Jo, and she and I went to look at headstones.

After the next family reunion, my kids, grandkids, and I went to Princeton City Park and I showed them where I played as a child. And the park still had the actual slide I slid on as a little boy! Up the ladder they all went, and then me. Thinking it might have been too much physical exertion, they begged me to get down. But I was having fun and continued up anyway.

Well, my boy parts are not where they used to be when I was little, and on the way down I smashed them when I landed, to say nothing of my flip phone (yes, although it was 2012, well into the smartphone technology age, I still had a flip phone!) which now lay on the ground in two pieces!

Right after the "nutcracker event" we visited the cemetery where my parents and other family members were buried. Together we looked for a nice shady plot under a tree, finally finding one in the older part of the property that might be available.

It seems kind of odd, but it was actually a lot of fun letting my offspring "meet" some of the people I grew up with and help choose the spot where my remains would be laid to rest. My grandson, who was in his early teens at the time, even remarked, "Well, this was not as sad as I thought it would be."

The entire experience brought me some comfort, knowing that I had accomplished a weighty task with ease and grace and perhaps made it a bit easier for those I would be leaving behind.

Sometime later my brother, Derald, who was on the board of the cemetery, learned that the shady plot we'd found was available. So he and I and my friend Bill went there together to give it another once-over, then I made the choice official.

We were getting it all ready. All I had to do to prepare for my smokin' hot body (cremation) was to put on a suit. And by "suit" I mean a t-shirt, shorts and one of my nicer pairs of flip-flops! And this may be a little TMI (Too Much Information), but no undies either!

Slowly but surely, I had been planting death seeds in the garden of my mind.

It wouldn't be long before they'd begin to sprout.

Chapter 26
<u>Digging up the Soil</u>

If I hadn't been so involved with energy work at this point in my life, I truly believe there would have been a totally different outcome to my diagnosis when the marbles hit the stairs. The "six-to-eight months to live" decree would have come to fruition, and the book you're currently reading would not have been written.

The Emotion Code chart and magnet work I was doing with Richard became mental and emotional shovels, helping me dig up the soil around decades-long fears: The fear of not being appreciated. The fear of rejection. The fear of not being wanted.

The biggest one laying at the root of it all was, *I'm not good enough.*

Then there was taking things personally. For example, somebody might be having a conversation nearby, and I'd start conjuring up some story in my mind that they were talking about me.

Take that time I went line dancing and was gripped with anxiety and so afraid people would see that I didn't have the steps right. Well, if you really think about it, how arrogant was I to think that the close to 40 other people there would be spending their time focusing on me and what I was or wasn't

179

doing? It was all a ridiculous story I'd made up and I was only torturing myself.

And as you might imagine, all of that fed right into my old victim stories which still come and go:

I'm fat. Who would want to be around somebody like me? If you knew I was gay you wouldn't like me. I'm not good enough.

The funny thing is, as time went on and more and more people found out I was gay, I realized there were only a few who broke away from me. The majority of them could really care less!

They just loved me for who I was.

Most of the time when Richard pointed out whatever he was seeing in my body, I'd instantly get a mental picture of an associated event from an earlier time in my life. It may have occurred way back, like in high school, or more recently and hadn't fermented for too long yet (says the recovering alcoholic!). Regardless of the life span of the lie I'd been telling myself, it was still in there kicking and screaming to get out!

These are just feelings, Richard said, but not the reality of the story I was making up. Again, all I needed to do was change what I said to my body.

As I moved through this cancer journey, some well-intentioned people unfortunately said some very hurtful things that stung.

One of them was, "You could stop making car payments, because by the time they come to get it..." Others, after my health began to improve, suggested that I was misdiagnosed. Even some of my "prayer warriors" later, when I was healed, said I should sue the doctor.

I was very shocked and disappointed that they would say things like that, but to combat any negative energy coming from those opinions (or about any other subject) Richard said I could simply listen while I imagined holding a rose between us as a symbol of protection.

"Just focus on that rose, John."

With some people I had to imagine holding up a whole bouquet of roses to keep their negative thoughts and energy away from me!

Reflecting on my early church childhood was bringing up a lot of emotions as well, some of it tied to scripture. For instance, in Luke 22:42 in the New Testament when Jesus was mentally preparing for his crucifixion he said, "Father, if you are willing, take this cup from me; yet not my will, but yours be done."

Now I've quoted and used this scripture since I was a young boy, but I'm not so sure I was being honest about what I was saying. Most of the time I'm sure I was really wanting things to go my way. So when the cancer showed up it was only natural that I would again start reciting this verse.

One morning, as I was praying it back to God, I realized again that only a very small part of me really meant "…but yours be done." So the next few days were spent thinking about how to deal with what I really believed to be my Truth. It was time for ole John to buckle down and get honest with God and himself, or to stop praying this particular prayer.

Right around that same time, one of the big events going on in our family was Mikey's high school graduation. This was a very special year for her and my daughter's family, and I didn't want the illness, or my death, to interrupt any of the festivities. So once again I reminded myself to let it go, and that whatever happened would be for the greatest and highest good of all concerned. We were always in a safe place with God.

The following spring I attended and thoroughly enjoyed all of Mikey's graduation celebrations, which also included taking her to lunch and to the nail salon where we both got pedicures and had a great Pa-Pa and Mikey talk about life.

The next day as her school band played the theme from *The Lion King,* "The Circle of Life," and "Pomp Circumstance," no one shed more tears of joy or smiled bigger than this proud ole Pa-Pa, knowing that my little Mikey is probably the only graduate who could say she enjoyed such a unique afternoon of pampering.

At that moment I remember thinking, "Life is good."

* * *

In between my in-person digging-up-the-soil appointments with Richard, there were things I was to do at home.

For example, if I experienced thoughts or sensations of not feeling good enough, or unappreciated, or fear, I would stop and say, "I'm just as good as anybody else. So, let go of that feeling. Just let it go."

As I kept practicing things like this, each time I went back for more therapy and magnet work the evidence of my error thinking was showing up less and less. And it wasn't long before my overall belief went from *IF* this change in my inner dialogue could cure the cancer to *This just might work and when it does, I'll be unstoppable!*

Now I wish I had an answer when I've heard people ask, "Why did God let [this or that] happen?" Or "I prayed for my loved one, and God let this happen anyway." And I really wish I could explain why others, including those I would consider much more spiritual than me, have passed away after battling some troubling diagnosis.

I'm not saying those people had less faith than me, or that they didn't fix all the right energy in the right places. But why did they die, and I didn't?

"Everybody has an expiration date. You were born with that," Richard said one day. "And when that time comes spiritual healing may make it easier, but it's not going to change that."

On the other hand, when people who know my story say, "God sure does love you!" Or "You're sure on God's side," that just sends chills down my spine. I believe that God loves a person who is dead or dying just as much as He loves me. And isn't God with us in everything? Well, I choose to believe that we're all on God's side. After all, we and God are one.

I know this cancer journey could have gone in a different direction. But it didn't. I was just doing what I could for me. And that's something we just have to learn: Just do what we can and leave it there.

Now I have to tell you that even with all of this great progress, I still had some garden weeds to pull. It was time to rewrite my childhood stories, the ones that had laid the foundation and created the space, I believe, for the cancer to enter my body in the first place.

I decided to do that by going back to Princeton.

First, I went to the site of our little country church which had long since closed and shouted and stormed through a lot of that early fire and brimstone programming I felt had led me down the path of error thinking.

I then went to several cemeteries to the graves of people I previously felt had hurt me or my family.

At my parents' final resting places I yelled and got rid of a lot of things I couldn't say to them way back when. Among them, "I'm gay, I'm gay, I'm gay!" If they were alive today these words might hurt and embarrass them. But I know I would still have received a lot of love and support.

And to their friends buried around them I threw in a few, "Hey look Robert, and Hazel, and Ralph, and Edna (the names are changed to protect their families' peace of mind!), I'm Queer! I'm Queer!"

My grandparents' graves were next, where I was mad as hell that they left before I could really get to know them.

After all of that ranting and raving, I felt more complete, though still a little guilty and shameful for what I'd just said and done.

Going back down to the homestead where I was raised gave me an opportunity to, literally, walk through a lot of my childhood experiences there.

The property was vacant, the house burning to the ground several years prior. But the barns, workshops, and garages were still standing. In the yard I reflected upon some inner work I had done in a workshop once after reading the book *Homecoming: Reclaiming and Healing Your Inner Child* by John Bradshaw. In it, he talks about the power of connecting with and nurturing our inner child in order to freely live in the present.

So I visualized my parents and this little guy sitting there. And I took that little boy aside and we had a good talk about life and what I'd learned. Then together we spoke to my parents,

185

telling them that Little Johnnie had to go and be the man he was born to be.

When we finished, I took him by the hand, and we walked away.

About a year or so later after doing more healing work—choosing love over resentment and recognizing the wonderful parts and not as much of the sadness and blame of my childhood—I stopped just outside the gate of the family cemetery.

After snapping off a handful of wild tiger lilies growing around the perimeter, I walked up to my parents' gravesite, laid the flowers there and said, "I'm sorry I had to do what I did when I was here before. But I had to be set free. Thank you for the good foundation you gave me, the good family roots. You did a wonderful job, and I'm happy now. I'm living the life I have always wanted. I love you, and I'll be back someday soon."

I was just digging up the soil, cleaning up my mental and emotional garden. And it was working.

Richard and I weren't the only ones seeing my great progress.

The sixth, then seventh, then eighth month of the predicted timeframe of my death had come and gone. And as I said before, at every monthly check-up the tumors had continued to shrink - without chemo, radiation, surgery, or even a baby aspirin!

Soon, those recheck visits stretched to about every three months.

A little over two years after the initial Stage 4 cancer diagnosis I was told the tumors were gone. Although the doctor didn't use these exact words, I did:

"I am cancer free."

Chapter 27
<u>Great is Thy Faithfulness</u>

Great is Thy faithfulness
O God my Father
There is no shadow of turning with Thee
Thou changest not
Thy compassions they fail not
As Thou hast been
Thou forever will be

There have been many times in my life when the lyrics to this song really spoke to me.

The first was in Lincoln when I worked as a press person at Back to the Bible. Moving on to greener pastures, I had recently gotten a job at another company where I would be the head of the department, which for me was a big deal, and I was very frightened about it.

On one of my last days there, I went into the chapel on the property and *Great is Thy Faithfulness* was playing. What I understood the words to express was that although I was changing—in this instance, a job—God was not. For me, hearing "Thou changest not" and "Thou forever will be" meant God was with me, and I would be OK.

From then on it seemed like whenever I would hear or see the lyrics of that song, something big was about to happen in my life. And whether it was something I wanted to happen, or something I did not, God would be faithful to me no matter what.

One day, many years later, I had some sort of major breakthrough during one of my therapy sessions. Once I'd left and gotten into my car, I turned on the radio (I listened to Christian radio stations back then), hoping to listen to *Great is Thy Faithfulness* on my way home. Well, it was 5 o'clock—prime rush hour driving time—so the station was right in the middle of the news. "I'll just wait," I thought, "because I'm sure it will play afterwards." As I sat at a traffic signal, waiting for the light to change, I heard the bells at a nearby church playing … you guessed it, *Great is Thy Faithfulness!*

It still gives me goosebumps when I think about every time something was going to challenge my faith, the different ways God let me know that He was still there. Even when I thought I had Him all figured out, something would remind me that maybe I needed to stop trying to do that, and let God do what God is going to do!

After the cancer diagnosis when things were looking grim and I thought I was dying, I really clung to the words of that song, affirming that God was going to be faithful to me regardless of what happened.

Great is Thy faithfulness
O God my Father
There is no shadow of turning with Thee
Thou changest not
Thy compassions they fail not
As Thou hast been
Thou forever will be

Great is Thy faithfulness
Great is Thy faithfulness
Morning by morning new mercies I see
And all I have needed Thy hands hath provided
Great is Thy faithfulness
Lord unto me

Pardon for sin
And a peace that endureth
Thine own dear presence to cheer
And to guide
Strength for today
and bright hope for tomorrow
Blessings all mine, with ten thousand beside

Great is Thy faithfulness
Great is Thy faithfulness
Morning by morning new mercies I see
And all I have needed Thy hands hath provided
Great is Thy faithfulness
Lord unto me

Chapter 28
<u>My New Spiritual Community</u>

Psychologist, spiritual teacher, and author Ram Dass has been quoted as saying, *"The next message you need is always right where you are."* And that's kind of how I would describe finding my next spiritual home.

Although I was happy attending MCC and so grateful for the love and support they'd given me over the years, especially to Beth and David during this cancer journey, I was beginning to feel like I wanted something more ... something deeper. It wasn't a big thunk on the head or anything like that. But just kind of a nudge, or a whisper, that I needed a quieter place to focus and meditate on spiritual growth.

Not too long after that, in 2017, Bill's former wife, Glenda, passed away and he asked me to attend the funeral with him. She had been a member of this place called the Center for Spiritual Living Kansas City (CSL), and Bill's son and Glenda's boyfriend were taking care of all of the arrangements. It was a first time visit for both of us.

The very first thing I remember after stepping through the doorway is this big, beautiful, Buddha statue resting on a square, white, waist-high block. Its presence was a little unsettling because it was so contrary to some of the old Baptist teachings I still had roaming around within me. Yet it still drew me in, and a peaceful feeling washed over me just by standing in front of it. And although we were there for a funeral which can be so sad and unsettling at times, it brought a lot of comfort and stillness to the occasion.

After her memorial was over, I knew I wanted to come back the next day for Sunday service. So on our way out I briefly glanced at one of their brochures to see what time it would start.

The next morning, I was very warmly greeted by one of the CSL volunteers as I explained how I knew about them, had found their environment to be very peaceful, and that I'd been looking for a new church and wanted to learn more. The man told me a little bit about them, handed me some literature, then pointed me toward the sanctuary.

Once again, the peacefulness of the Buddha drew me in.

At almost every church I've ever been to, there was almost a ball game atmosphere to it before the main service started. The people were rowdy, there were lots of loud voices going back and forth across the room, and kids were running all over the place.

But not at CSL.

The people seemed genuinely happy to be there, and although they were milling about talking to each other, there was a lot of stillness in the air.

Another thing that caught my eye—and I still marvel at it now—is that this was also the first church I'd ever been to where the people, on their own, filled in the front of the church first!

What I'd always seen was congregants filling in the seats in the back of the sanctuary, then the middle, and lastly the front. Witnessing this seat selection process in reverse at CSL told me: *Something wonderful is going on here and people want to be a part of it.*

I took it as another good sign that instead of seeing a lot of "grey or blue-haired people," I noticed a wide range of ages and races, singles and couples, gay and straight, and families with children. CSL was definitely not a church where the congregants were withering on the vine.

Instead of a traditional church choir, CSL had a band with two vocalists, a drummer, bass guitarist, keyboard player, and pianist. Right before things got started, I saw a man named Mark Hayes walk up to the piano. I knew who he was because he'd written and performed several different musical arrangements for the HMC, and he'd also attended and played at Broadway Church, so I knew the music would be great.

And oh my, was it!

For one thing, the vibration was a lot calmer than what I was used to, which was musicians playing so loudly you couldn't hear what the vocalists were singing! But even with that more tolerable volume, I have to admit that at first the songs sounded a little strange to me. They were very different from the typical "Sweet By and By" kind of thing, or heavy burdensome songs about some horrible time in our lives, "but God's going to pull us through" type of lyrics.

They were singing cheerful, encouraging messages about living in the present moment. Not in the past, or in the future, but in the *now*.

The lesson that Sunday, given by Sr. Minister Rev. Mike Irwin, also reflected that same in-the-present-moment theme. I don't remember the exact topic or words used, but I know that I went home with a new, practical "spiritual tool" I could use to improve my life *that day.* It was all about how, no matter what's going on in your life, to *be here now* (which is also the name of a book written by Ram Dass).

When it came time for meditation, I felt perfectly comfortable. I was accustomed to doing it by myself, Bill and I had meditated together on several occasions, and Richard and I had spent time in the silence many times — just the two of us and as part of the groups he used to facilitate in his home. But I'd never experienced meditation as part an overall church service.

A lot of times when you go to church, especially as a first timer, you sometimes want to get out of there as fast as you can. Even the regulars want to get on with their weekend! But this first Sunday visit, and every time since, I noticed how the folks at CSL weren't doing this. They were engaged in lively conversations both inside and out in the parking lot, and to me this spoke of a true desire to create fellowship and maybe friendships down the line.

After that experience I was pretty sure this was where I wanted to land. However, just to be sure, I wanted to give it several more visits to learn more about what went on there. I learned that the Center for Spiritual Living Kansas City was originally founded by Dr. Chris Michaels in 1990 as part of the global Centers for Spiritual Living organization which has over 500 centers worldwide. The organization was founded in the early 20th century by Dr. Ernest Holmes, a New Thought writer, teacher, and leader.

Dr. Holmes believed that all of the world religions and faith traditions had a shared thread of truth running through them, and because of this, no person, group, or religion had exclusive rights to one truth. And he used that thread to create principles called "Science of Mind" which are followed by people all over the world.

At CSL, their core values are Love, Healing, Oneness, Abundance, Spiritual Growth, Service, and Diversity. And they express it on their website like this:

At Center for Spiritual Living Kansas City (CSLKC), we want you to feel welcome just as you are, regardless of age, race, religion, gender, gender identification, who you love, who you vote for, education or income. You do not have to give up your idea of God or your personal faith in order to join us. You are welcome even if you are questioning your faith.

Our music is upbeat with a positive message. We teach a relevant and practical spirituality that works in everyday life.

Our goal is that you feel more hopeful and encouraged when you leave than when you arrived.

What is noticeably absent from CSL is any dogma or rules. Although they do reference the Bible, they believe that everything Jesus could do and be, we could do and be also, and that he was a "way shower"—an example—and not the exception. CSL also incorporates beliefs and teachings from sacred eastern texts like Buddhism, Taoism, Hinduism, and others as resources for spiritual growth that honor all paths to God.

Before you knew it, I started going to both Sunday services – the 9 a.m. Spiritual Practice Service (30 minutes of reflective music, a little bit of a message, and a lengthy meditation), followed by the 10 a.m. Celebration Service I'd enjoyed before.

Before, after, and in between the two, CSL offers opportunities for prayer with their Prayer Practitioners whose roles are in stark contrast to "The Invitation" I grew up with where we'd all stand up and sing "Just as I Am" while the preacher walked up and down the aisle begging and pleading people to come to Jesus (just to be fair, as the years went by I'd seen this kind of soften down a bit and not feel, to me anyway, so "circus-like"). Or the only option you had was to meet the preacher at the front of the church after service if you wanted to pray with him about something.

Another big difference is that CSL's Prayer Practitioners don't pray *for* you, rather *with* you. They're there as part of the spiritual support system, really listening to any challenges or wonderful happenings you want to share and offering affirmative prayers that help you connect to whatever you call your Higher Power. What I really like and appreciate, and what I've heard from each one of them, is the gentle guidance toward a continued openness to what I know is best and true for me in my life. That I am light, love, and "a perfect expression of God, entitled to a life of love and joy" – the last part the affirmation the congregation says together at the end of the main Celebration Service.

There's no begging or finding the right words to convince some god "out there" to rescue me, or to bestow me with the good I'm seeking. Yes, they're saying a prayer, but it's not an advisory prayer.

Every time, no matter what issue I've brought to any of them, I walked away feeling like I'd really been heard, am connected to something greater than myself, and, like the Sunday morning lessons, that I had a new, practical spiritual tool I could use in my daily life.

When Rev. Mike or Rev. Mary Lowry, CSL's Office Administrator (and former Sr. Minister at the CSL in Las Cruces, NM), aren't giving the lesson, they bring in other great speakers from different faith traditions, ages, races, and gender identifications, each one offering wonderful insights into their life stories and how they intersect with their current levels of spiritual awareness and beliefs. It all ties into CSL's motto, I guess you could say, where "everyone has a seat at the table."

Although a lot of the speakers' experiences are very different from my own, I can still identify the common thread stretching through every faith tradition: the belief in a higher power.

The youth department themes reflect that diversity of thought as well. Whether it's the topic or spiritual principles culled from the speakers' presentations, or a theme centered around a celebration or practice such as Día de los Muertos (Day of the Dead), Ramadan, Passover, Easter, Christmas, the solstice, Kwanzaa, and so forth, the youth department staff creates age appropriate teachings, games, crafts, videos and the like as a foundation for discussion here and at home with family and friends.

It makes me so happy to know that the kids at CSL are being exposed to a broader view of the world around them and provided an opportunity to think about what they believe, and what doesn't resonate with them, instead of being told "how things are" like many of us were when we were at a young age.

It wasn't long before the twice a month, Wednesday night "A Place to Pause" service (a mid-week "tune-up" much like the 9 a.m. Spiritual Practice Service on Sundays) also became part of my regular attendance routine.

Once I started enrolling in their classes—some designed just for expansion of spiritual awareness and knowledge, others for those who want to become certified as a Prayer Practitioner or as part of ministerial licensing—I was more easily able to let go of some of what I considered to be the false teachings from my past, and instead grasp onto a greater, higher level of thinking Truths (yes, Truths with a capital "T").

Sometimes sharing your feelings or struggles with a group of strangers is very intimidating or scary. And people often put on airs, so others won't think less of them. But the sharing in the classes I attend here are very unpretentious.

For example, I distinctly remember going around the room sharing what we were grateful for. And not one of the people there gave an "I need to impress you," flowery, word-filled, Thanksgiving Day type of list. It was more about expressing gratitude to God for the people and circumstances that have brought us to and made us who we are now.

As far as being a gay man, I could state that here as easily as I could say, "I like my coffee black" - without any guilt or fear that I wouldn't be accepted.

It was also in these classes that I got to know Rev. Mike and Rev. Mary on a more intimate level, and to enjoy the spiritual gifts they have to share with others.

I met Rev. Mike during my first visit to CSL. At the end of each service he stands at the door to greet people, and despite the long line of folks waiting to talk to him he still took the time to talk and listen to me. It was so unlike other churches where it seemed like this was an expected part of the minister's role and they just had to grin and bear it. But Rev. Mike has a very calm, authentic personality that really appeals to people. And when we spoke, he was very genuine about asking about me and how I'd found CSL and invited me back anytime.

In the years since then during hospital-stays for some non-cancer related health issues I was experiencing, Rev. Mike would send a card with a note saying that if I needed anything, not to hesitate to call him. He didn't just show up (and while my hospital gown might have been open to boot!) because he thought that was what he was supposed to do. But I knew that if I really did need him, he'd there.

He also often came to the "A Place to Pause" meditation on Wednesday nights, not in a leadership capacity, rather simply to sit beside the rest of us in the silence. To me that meant he was also making it a priority to get a mid-week reset along his spiritual path.

By the time I got to CSL I'd had some exposure to female ministers, and it took me some time to be able to really listen to them because I was so accustomed to preaching from men. But women ministers did intrigue me because they had a kind of more emotional and insightful connection with people than most men.

At CSL, I found Rev. Mary to be such a joy! She has a quirky personality and a lot of wisdom and experiences to share. And it seemed to me like she connected the dots between what she taught and real human emotions and reality. It was again, another perspective that brought more meaning to what I was learning.

Using the basic principles of Science of Mind, CSL offers classes like Self-Mastery, the emerging of the true self; Beyond Limits, how to live without boundaries through affirmative prayer, creative thinking, setting intentions, meditation, and other focuses; and Practical Mysticism, designed to help us deepen our own awareness of the Divine Reality of all, among others.

Another on-going class series I really enjoy here is Visioning, taught by Virginia Firestone, one of the Prayer Practitioners. In it we learn how to expand our awareness of ourselves and our connection to that Higher Power in order to manifest what we desire to experience in our lives.

During the Sunday service, sometimes the music team will sing this song called, "Let Go of the Shore" written by New Thought musician Karen Drucker (she also wrote a book by the same name).

In it she says that we needn't be afraid of letting go, and that by doing so, allowing the waters to carry us "into the mystery"—the unknown—we will ultimately connect with our inner resources. It is there that we'll find our strength.

The not knowing is OK. Just let go of the shore.

What comes to mind when I hear it is this crystal-clear river where you can see all the way to the bottom. And me and everyone else in it are peacefully floating along.

But sometimes I'll suddenly be gripped by fear and think I need to regain control, and my vision changes to me trying to latch onto the grass, weeds, or brush along the shore so I won't be dragged out to sea and drown. When I do this, a lot of dirt from my past comes up. It's so symbolic of how I'd been living most of my life.

In the visioning class I am learning that letting go of the shore is actually how the magic in our life happens; how what we want to manifest shows up.

With everything I keep learning, I feel like I really want to focus on why I'm here on earth at this particular time in history. I know I've been drawn into a ministry of healing—similar to my massage therapy practice—and if that centers around helping people with a very serious prognosis like I once had, or being with somebody that just needs an ear to listen or a shoulder to cry on, I want to be that open channel of love for them.

I'm pulling away from the old "I'm not good enough" stories, knowing that I'm really OK and here to do good works on the planet.

When I found CSL I was so thirsty to go deeper in my life, and they were definitely quenching that thirst. The more I heard, the more I wanted to learn. At the same time I realized that the more I knew, the more I knew I didn't know!

The one thing I did know, however, was that CSL was definitely my new spiritual home.

Chapter 29
<u>Calamity Jane</u>

The parade took place on Saturday, September 21, 2019 as part of the three-day, annual Calamity Jane Days celebration. It is part of Princeton's claim to fame, you may recall me saying earlier, as the 1852 birthplace of this Wild West-era, whiskey drinkin', quick of wit and tongue, sharp-shootin' woman tough enough to run with the likes of Wild Bill Hickok and his gang.

The invitation for every generation of the Delameter family to participate as Grand Marshals came from the Chamber of Commerce and the good news was shared with everyone at our annual family reunion that August.

I was so excited and thought it was so cool because I'd been in the parade a few years earlier as part of my 50-year high school reunion celebration. Now this opportunity had shown up and the more I thought about it, the more honored and humbled I became that they would ask our family to do such a thing.

Everybody of course wanted to participate but getting organized at first was like herding a bunch of cats! There were just so many of us. But once we got started, things really took off and it was so nice to see how we all contributed our unique gifts and talents.

For our "floats" we found plenty of tractors, wagons, and hay bales for people to sit on, we chose a patriotic theme for our rides, decorating them in red, white, and blue banners, and we bought little hand flags for folks to wave. We also had a "poster night" where heartfelt remembrances of loved ones we had lost—parents, siblings, spouses, children, and grandchildren—were created to hang on the sides.

Our "15 minutes of fame" also included, smack dab in the middle of the Princeton Chamber of Commerce Facebook page, this post:

> "The CJ Parade 2019 Grand Marshals are
> The Delameter Family."

When I really thought about it, I realized there were at least seven generations of Delameters that were, or still are, being raised in Princeton. So, this Grand Marshal (one of my brother Derald's great grandsons kept saying we were going to be the "Grand Marshmallows!") honor bestowed upon us for being there all those years was really significant.

There is something for everyone at the Calamity Jane Day celebration: a classic car show, rotary breakfast at the senior center, kids pedal pull, and a teen dance.

For years, a man named Danny Hagan would bring extra tools and parts from his mechanic shop to have on hand should anyone's vehicle run into a problem. After he passed, Princeton decided to honor him with a community-wide Danny Hagan Memorial Tractor Cruise, and a lot of our family members took part.

It seemed like hundreds of donations came in for the cakewalk—light and dark chocolate, crunchy carrot, fluffy vanilla crème, thick strawberry swirl, buttery yellow pound, and more—some store bought, others homemade family recipes.

Two really cute events were the Princess and Prince Pageant for three and four-year olds, and the Kindergartners and First Graders competed for the title of Little Miss Calamity Jane or Little Wild Bill.

The teenaged Miss Calamity Jane Pageant takes place the week before with about a dozen contestants all dolled up in shimmering gowns and high heels strutting their stuff on stage at the Princeton United Methodist Church in front of family, friends, peers, and no doubt, male admirers.

There was also plenty of music and entertainment on the bandstand that year by the Real Beals, the Ambassador Band, Hired Gun, and the Katty Wampus Band, karaoke by the football team, fancy footwork by the Mic-O-Say Dancers, and an all-school concert, among other acts - all part of the local talent so much a part of our little community. And there was plenty of dancing too!

An annual favorite with some of my relatives performing in it, was the Melodrama play at the Cow Palace, and more local talent was on display at the quilt show. Then there were the customary inflatables for the kids, an old-time photo booth, and homemade ice cream served by the Chamber of Commerce staff.

Another big highlight of the weekend was the annual Homecoming football game, my alma mater Princeton Tigers victorious over the Milan Wildcats in a thriller with a final score of 24-25.

The official parade start was on Saturday at 1 p.m. with the National Anthem. The long line of participants began at the Mercer County Fair Barn, wound its way in and around town, then went north of the Princeton Square where it made a big U-turn, came back south, and kept going to the final stop in the middle of the square.

When my mother was in her early high school years, she lived and worked as a housekeeper and cook at a large home called The Bailey House (named after the owners). The house sat at the top of the hill at the corner of College and Main Street, and about three blocks away my father owned a butcher shop. Because of their close proximity, I assume that's how their paths eventually crossed. So, it was kind of amazing to me that about a century later there were at least 88 of us in a parade on the very street where their relationship began. Oh how do we beget! That's at least one part of the Bible we all believed in!

Hyde, Foster's great grandson, and Ollie, Jo's great grandson, who were toddlers, were the youngest. The oldest, at age 95, was Lenora, H.A.'s widow.

As the Grand Marshals, we were positioned near the front of the line, and as you can imagine, with so many of us, we had a lot of tractors and wagons. We probably had enough to make our own full-length parade! The first vehicle for each branch of the family tree was for the siblings and their spouses, then our children and spouses, followed by our grandchildren, then great grandchildren. We also came up with a sort of coding system where each sibling branch wore the same color t-shirts and caps.

It's kind of funny because after going through all of that organizing, the temperamental Missouri weather took a turn for the worse and it rained down on us for most of the parade. So we all had to put raincoats on, and no one saw our colorful matching after all! This parade had been going on for over 50 years, and I'd been to probably about 30 of them. This was the only time I remember it raining.

Despite this, I sat on a picnic bench on an open trailer pulled behind a bright red McCormick Farmall tractor, hefting myself up there on a ramp someone came up with so the "senior people" could get on without too much of a struggle. On it, posters of Mom and Dad, H.A., George, Clay, Lillian, Foster, Jerrie, and any of their spouses who had also passed away hung on the sides, while the *Stars and Stripes Forever* boomed loudly and proudly from our music box speakers.

And when we passed by one of the businesses on the square, we saw a tribute display with a little bit of our family history and accomplishments on it.

In the rest of the parade there were tractors, and trucks, and SUVs, and trailers, and pony drawn buggies, and floats representing just about every school, organization, and business in town: The Princeton R-5 Homecoming Court, Al's Bees, Girdner Post & Lumber, Pearl's Residential Care, EverCare Pharmacy, Vit-A-Zine Farm Supply, the Mercer County Extension of the University of Missouri, the Sheriff's office, county ambulance company, and the Mercer Fire Protection District. There was even an appearance by the Kansas City Chiefs mascot, KC Wolf, which for our little town was a big deal!

Because of the rain the beautiful pageant queen had to sit in the front seat instead of in the back of her "chariot," a Ford F150 truck, so the downpour wouldn't muss up her dress or hair adorned with a glistening tiara.

All of the marching bands were forced to cover up their instruments (except for the tubas) with see-through plastic bags! Their sounds, however, were still just as sweet.

Although the crowds were a little smaller than usual, and in the end the procession lasted only about 30 minutes, we definitely didn't let it rain on our parade! We held strong and it was a real joy for me to see so many generations of my family together at one time.

Later that afternoon we gathered at my late brother Jerrie's home, sitting in the garage and under big tents to share smoked pork sandwiches, hot dogs, baked beans, potato salad, chips, and in true Delameter-style, plenty of desserts too!

The "Best of" awards were presented that evening with honors given for Best Tractor, Organization Float, Original Tractor,

Business Float, Horse-Drawn Entry, Classic Car, Dressed Youth Rider, Most Unusual Entry (that went to the Melodrama actors, of course!), and so on.

Looking through the pictures people took over the days and weeks to follow made me really start thinking about my roots. And I felt a real appreciation for the "village" in which I was raised, and the support that village gave me in my youth and is still giving me now.

Over the years I've continued to go back to enjoy, or follow on Facebook, family activities including cheerleading and football games, dance performances, elementary, middle, high school, and college graduations, engagements and weddings, birthday parties and homegoing celebrations of life. Whether near or far, Princeton has always been a part of me, and me a part of it. And it always brings to mind that saying, *The more things change, the more they stay the same.*

You can see it in the big family picture we took before the parade, and in our faces when we received a congratulatory plaque from the Chamber of Commerce for the contributions our family had made to the community over the years. It was a wonderful moment for us all and I know Momma and Daddy would have been very proud.

Calamity Jane herself might have liked it too!

I suppose my life has come full circle. But I would have missed a great deal of it if the doctor's six-to-eight-months-to-live prediction, or my unwillingness or inability to dig up the weeds in my life, had come to pass.

Chapter 30
<u>Eva</u>

There is a lot to be said about what forgiving does for you. And how not doing it can eat you alive.

Sometimes people who know me well ask questions like, "If you were gay, why did you get married?" Or "How could you have been unfaithful during your marriage?" Or "Do you regret some of the things you've done?"

I guess they think that if I'd had an inkling I was gay, I shouldn't have deceived Eva (and everyone else for that matter) by joining in holy matrimony.

I respond by explaining, or reminding, people about the culture in the late '50s and early '60s when people were raised to believe that after graduating from high school you either went to college or got a job, and got married. That was it. That's how we thought life was supposed to work.

Now, it is true that I thought early on in my life, prior to Eva, that there was something wrong or different about me. But the bottom line is I didn't know for sure what it was. The possibility of being gay wouldn't have been something I would've known or understood. It was just that I was always called "Sissy" and "Momma's Boy" and other names that this boy's momma would not be very proud of if I said them publicly!

And even if I might have known I was gay when I was young, admitting it, dating boys (or going into the big city to find some), were never options for me.

So, based on that social programming and my 17-year old wisdom, I went for the marriage thing. I really thought that once I had sex with a woman my whole way of thinking would change – that I'd be drawn toward a woman and think she was attractive, just like I felt about boys. And by attractive, I mean getting goosebumps and a tingling in my spine when I was around them. I didn't know what that was, but it felt oh so good! I knew I didn't get that feeling about girls like the boys did, and it seemed like there was something very wrong with that.

I would hear what the guys were saying about them—the cat calls, bragging about their wild sexual experiences, or at least their genuine interest. But I didn't have any of that.

As far as marriage, when it came down to it, Eva and I were just two kids trying to put a home together in an era when that was just what you did. There were so many things about life neither of us knew about yet, and we felt there was no one we could turn to for help.

As you might imagine, after Eva and I divorced, each time we saw each other—from time to time at work, at any kind of family function, etc.—things were always strained and awkward. There was still a lot of hurt, on both of our parts, and seeing each other just brought all those old feelings back up again.

About four or five years after signing on the dotted line I attended the Landmark Forum, the highly successful program designed to help people bring about positive, permanent shifts in the quality of their lives (and I've continued attending their seminars over the years).

In one of the sessions they talked about going back to those we had wronged to "clean it up," take ownership of the role we played in whatever the situation, apologize, and forgive.

Eva was the first person who came to mind.

So the following Monday at work I went by her office, gently sat down in the chair beside her, and offered a deep, truly heartfelt apology for my behavior when we were married.

After listening intently to what I was saying she responded, "I forgive you. It takes two to do things like this."

That short and honest conversation opened the channels of acceptance more than I could have possibly imagined.

As the years progressed, things really started to come together. And when we did see each other our relationship got better.

For example, at our son David's wedding rehearsal, Eva and her new husband, Ben, were practicing walking down the aisle. I was next, and when I got to where they were, I said, "Where am I supposed to sit?" Eva just giggled, elbowed him in the side and said, "Scoot over, Ben. I'll sit between you!"

Now that may sound like a simply nice and cute gesture, but the following night at the actual wedding when my son came out to be married, he saw his mother, father, and stepfather not only sitting beside each other, but at peace with each other. It made all the difference in the world—to him and to us.

When Beth and her family came back to Kansas City for a visit, we always tried to have some kind of family gathering. One time, at a picnic at my house, Eva and I were in the kitchen and my partner at the time and Ben were sitting on the couch laughing about something. Eva looked over and said to me, "Do you think they're comparing notes?"

On another occasion Eva called out, "Honey!" and both Ben and I responded at the same time, "Yes?" We had a good laugh about that one!

They were hilarious moments, and I was glad we could get to a place of mutual acceptance and friendship.

Years later, Eva unfortunately started to develop Alzheimer's. And as we know, that's when a lot of our day-to-day and earlier in life memories really started to fade. After Ben passed away, I felt honored to be around to help fill in some of the missing pieces.

In the summer of 2017, our grandson in Illinois was going to play the role of Garvin in a community theater production of *Footloose*. I already had plans to go and Eva said she wanted to go too, so I took her.

There are two very wonderful things I remember about that 8-hour car ride.

The first is when we left Princeton.

As we drove out of town and through Mercer County, I pointed out things along the way – like where my parents and brother, Derald, lived, and she seemed to remember them.

As we got to Chillicothe, MO I asked if she remembered that her cousin had pastored a church here. Right away she started squealing and giggling like a little girl, put her hand over her mouth, and said, "Oh, that's where we spent 'that night!'" Yes, we had spent our wedding night there, attending her cousin's church the next day. It was where, 55 years ago our honeymoon dreams had been crushed. But now it was nothing but a sweet memory for her.

When we got to Hannibal, MO we stopped for lunch. Afterwards, when I drove down by the Mark Twain Riverboat, I saw a cruise excursion just about to raise the gangplank. I hustled into the office, told the lady at the counter that "my wife" had always wanted to go on one of those, and now she had Alzheimer's.

"Is there any way we can get onboard?" I asked.

"Yes, and we will wait for you," the nice and understanding lady responded.

I quickly bought two tickets, went back to the car, and said to Eva, "How would you like to go on one of those riverboat cruises?" And she again squealed with delight, just like a little girl.

Throughout the day as we continued on toward Illinois, we did a lot of laughing, crying, and holding hands.

Over the years what I've seen when Alzheimer's really starts to take root is a continuous reverting back toward childhood. At that point with us, Eva's world was somewhere around upper grade school or early high school. Her mind was in a consistently blissful state; her memories now only anchored in the sweet times we'd had together as a couple.

We didn't know it then, but the week Eva stayed behind in Illinois after our grandson's play, she and Beth coming back to Princeton together on the train, would be her last visit at their home. This road trip would also be the last time Eva and I spent together that wasn't interrupted more with repeating things she didn't remember, than talking about those she did.

She remembers us only a little bit now.

During one of my visits to the retirement home were Eva now lives, she was carrying around a baby doll, feeding it with a bottle. And while I was there, she let me hold it. Later, on the way back to Kansas City I jokingly thought, *Is she going to hit me up with a paternity suit?* (I know, I ain't right!)

To keep Eva from getting up and falling, her bed had been lowered to about 18-inches off the floor. On two occasions when the kids, one of the grandkids and I came to visit, they very sweetly knelt down beside her—stroking her hair and face, sharing comforting words, and just being close to their momma and grandma. It really struck me that after all those years, going back to when they were little, how she loved, and held, and cooed, and nurtured them. And now they were able to do that for her.

Life sure does come full circle.

As her wandering words came and went, one of the very clear things she asked me again was, "What did I do wrong?" And that just broke my heart because I knew she was talking about the day, decades ago, when I told her I was gay, and she had asked what she "did wrong" that caused it.

After all these years, as far as we'd come in the acceptance of who we were in our relationship—then and over time—and through all of the healing that came from it, she had somehow still held onto that one disappointment.

The only thing I could think of to say was, "You're just fine. Everything is just fine." Just sitting there holding her seemed to be what she really needed.

So, going back to the regret question, yes, I do have regrets.

I regret that I moved through life as a socially ignorant young man that didn't know what I didn't know.

217

I regret that I had no idea how to function as a husband in a marriage, and I feel bad that Eva and our kids had to experience that.

I regret and am sorry about the pain I caused both of our families. I was just doing the best I could.

But regrets will get me nowhere now.

Forgiveness, on the other hand, is a liberating experience that will ultimately set us free.

Forgiveness takes effort.

Forgiveness takes practice.

Forgiveness takes time, patience, compassion, and grace.

Thank you, Eva, for all the wonderful years we did have together and for how we still did our best to become friends and the best parents and grandparents for our family.

Chapter 31
A.C. – After Cancer

It is now September 2020 – eight years after the glass marbles hit the stairs and my life seemed to be crashing down around me.

Eight years since staring death in the face and getting ready for a fast-approaching end.

This cancer journey has been about far more than my physical health. It has been an on-going learning experience about self-discovery, forgiveness, love, faith, letting go, connection, understanding, and gratitude.

My overall spiritual growth has been the central part of that. I've been able to more closely look at my early religious upbringing, decide what parts still work for me, bring in new thoughts, ideas, beliefs, and ways of being, and chart new paths for growth.

But I don't see that growth as just for me. I see it as that spark of Divinity I'm learning about at CSL; the perfect expression of God that I am and how I share that spark towards the healing and spiritual growth of the planet. How we can all come together, let go of everything that no longer serves us, and set our spirits free.

Even now, I still struggle with how to explain surviving Stage 4 Cancer without chemo, radiation, or surgery (and don't forget without that baby aspirin too!). And it bears repeating that I'm not a doctor and would never tell anyone not to consult a medical professional.

There's no way to guarantee that positive thoughts can cure any physical condition. But I do know that we can *always* give healing energy to it, which can open channels to better overall mental, emotional, and spiritual health and wellness.

I know this cancer journey could have gone in a different direction. But it didn't. I just did what I could for me. And that's something we just have to learn. Just do what we can and leave it there.

Before the Grim Reaper showed up at my door, I may have baulked at a lot of things in life.

After I sent it on its way, *everything* in my life takes on new meaning.

Some of the first things I wanted to do when I got the diagnosis was sell the house I was living in, get all my affairs in order, and clean up the past family and other relationship messes I'd created. And it's still an on-going thing for me to say I'm sorry to anyone I feel I may have hurt in the past.

I've always loved and tried to attend and enjoy as many of the special events in my family's life as I could — my daughter, son, and grandkids' school activities, church functions, holiday programs, theater productions, marching band performances, debate contests, and birthday celebrations. My siblings' anniversary parties, special career and community recognitions, and other activities are in that mix as well.

I now have a new zest, love, and gratitude for being there. As I unearthed the negative clutter I believe was feeding the cancer, I also removed the blockage keeping me from being fully present to those precious moments in their lives. Now when I'm with people, any people, I feel the experience more deeply than before.

On the first Sunday in January every year, CSL, like many churches and spiritual centers around the world, offers a White Stone Ceremony, an ancient ritual dating back to Biblical days. It comes from Revelation 2:17 in which the Apostle John is writing what he believes to be a direct command from Jesus to record his words:

"He who has an ear, let him hear what the Spirit says to the churches. To him who overcomes, to him I will give some of the hidden manna, and I will give him a white stone, and a new name written on the stone which no one knows but he who receives it."

During the ceremony we pray and meditate, asking our Higher Power to guide us toward a word or words to write on our stone. In this way, it symbolizes starting over with a clean slate, releasing ourselves from the bondage of the outer world, and instead listening for the "still, small voice" within. The word or words written set the intention for our highest and greatest good throughout the coming year.

The guidance that came to me was the word "Oneness." And as this year—2020—has progressed with all going on with the COVID-19 pandemic, escalating racial tensions, and our divisive and broken political system, I've become more aware of that Oneness and need for connection to each other.

For me, it shows up in many ways.

As an example, when I give a massage, I'm paid with money my clients have earned with their talents. And I in turn gratefully accept that money, using it to support myself and help others.

When out in my garden, I feel that connection between the water I'm giving the flowers, which connects them to the earth, bringing oxygen, color, and life to the insects, birds, and animals that feed from them. My focus is not on the weeds nearby that need to be pulled, rather on the joy the flowers bring to all who love and admire them.

And I know that the energy, words, thoughts, and prayers I put out to those around me who are going through challenges are all part of affirming that their highest and greatest good is unfolding.

To me, these things are a savoring of the moments and an interweaving of Oneness; a giant web that's not only connecting us but holding us together.

After Cancer, I've noticed it's a lot easier for me to part with tangible things than it was before. I'm not as prone to holding onto decades-old childhood mementos just for the sake of having them. Gifting them to someone who will love and cherish them feels more peaceful and fulfilling.

After Cancer, I'm more loving and forgiving of myself, to the point that sometimes when I think I've strayed off-course I say to myself, "Oh Sweetie! That's not the way I wanted to do that!" instead of using self-inflicted hurtful names.

After Cancer, I'm much better at not taking things personally, I no longer feel the need to defend my words or actions, and I'm more accepting of other points of view. I love that saying by the famous essayist Anaïs Nin, "We don't see the world as it is, we see it as we are." It just puts everything in perspective.

After Cancer, I'm much more comfortable in my own skin and have no problem doing things alone like eating out, going to the movies, or other activities. My old victim story, even while enjoying the solo time was, "People might think I have no friends." Now I don't even give it a second thought.

After Cancer, I see myself not as the "new me" but the *real me* who is now free to express myself in any way I see fit. I've learned to make happen what I want to have happen. Deciding why I want to do something, what's important, and what's not, makes all the difference in how I live my life.

After Cancer, in this deeper relationship with myself and with God, I feel a much greater connection to everyone and everything around me. My earlier guardedness and shallowness in life only created more guardedness and shallowness in my experiences. Letting all of that go has cast a wider net of love, inclusiveness, and Oneness.

After Cancer, Oneness and forgiveness have become far more important than anything to me.

After Cancer, I feel like you and I are truly worthy of God's love, acceptance, grace, and mercy.

After Cancer, my message is as simple as this:

Let go of the past, reach for the future, but at all times live in the present.

Cherish the moments you have because you never know when they will be your—or someone else's—last.

Stage 4 Cancer: Verdict or Choice
Despite the prognosis, I chose to live.

Chapter 32
But the Greatest of these is LOVE

One of the reasons for writing this book and exposing my "dirty laundry" was to stand skinlessly before you in order that you might also find healing in mind, body, and spirit.

However, little did I know that putting my complete life on paper would also unearth more healing than I could have ever imagined.

When I re-read this book now, I see that there were so many subconscious beliefs about myself, both before and after my birth, that I've allowed to direct my way of thinking and living.

As children, maybe just to survive in our family of origin, we create what we feel are safe havens to make it through, and they serve us well at the time. I get that. But now as adults, we need to reexamine those decisions and make adjustments accordingly.

For me it was letting go of the "stinkin' thinkin'" about myself, as well as the many forms of "protection" I'd built around me. By trying to shut out the bad, I was also shutting out the good, making it difficult to love and feel loved.

Unearthing takes time, but it is very doable.

A "real life" includes connection, intimacy, and vulnerability. A willingness to engage and be fully present when in dialogue with others. An acknowledgement that no matter what is said, I may want—or even need—to change my opinion or way of thinking about an issue.

FAITH, HOPE, PEACE, and LOVE light the way.

FAITH

There are two important parts to Faith: Belief and Commitment.

When you believe something to be true, then you wholeheartedly commit your life to it. Whether it's climate change, healthy eating, being of service to others, or a particular spiritual path, you jump in with both feet, knowing that the blessings will be greater than any challenges that may arise.

We must have faith in ourselves and commit to being the best that we can be, because deep down we KNOW we are worth the effort.

HOPE

Not just the hope that something will work but expecting— with absolute confidence—that it will.

To some this may sound like Faith, and I suppose in some ways it is. But to me Hope is a stronger grasping of expectation—of trusting, even if I can't see how—that my greater good is always unfolding.

PEACE

Peace is creating harmony within ourselves and in our relationship with others. We say, "Peace on Earth," "Live in Peace," and "Rest in Peace" when someone passes away. Yet there is more turmoil on our planet today than ever before.

So where is this peace that we all seem to be looking for? I believe it is within each of us and like Faith and Hope, it has to be unearthed from the inside out.

LOVE

I believe that everything comes down to LOVE.

LOVE can take many forms: devotional, romantic, bliss, unconditional ... all of these are important and show up in many areas of our lives. But deep down in the roots, our very existence, our essence—is LOVE.

It's a LOVE rooted in our creator—no matter what you call it—that sent us to this earthly plane to spread our inner light to LOVE ourselves, others, and the planet.

Learning to LOVE myself has brought major transformation in the simplest and most profound ways in every area of my life.

Yes, all of this does kind of sound like I'm going through a midlife crisis but remember that I'm already 77. So if this is a midlife crisis, that means I'm going to live to be over 150 years old. And if this is true, I intend to look and feel fabulous every step of the way!

But more than anything, this newly unearthed SELF-LOVE has opened my heart to reach out to others. It has allowed me to be more understanding and really listen to their joys and pains and be very present for them.

SELF-LOVE may sound selfish but like traveling by air, in the event of an emergency, you have to put your oxygen mask on first before you can help others.

* * *

At the time of this writing, our world is in deep turmoil with the COVID-19 pandemic, racial tension, a crushing financial recession, and government leadership that has failed us.

But my friends, LOVE can and will change all of this.

LOVE starts by loving yourself. It may take some time, but you're worth it.

If we don't tap into LOVE, we don't have LOVE to give. Without it we're just playing games with our words, deeds, and emotions. As such, little (if any) transformation will take place.

As I said before, LOVE is not the "new" me … it's the *real me.*

LOVE, along with FAITH, HOPE, and PEACE will slowly but surely transform our planet.

LOVE always wins.

What I'd like to leave with you are the words from 1 Corinthians 13:

If I speak in the tongues of men or of angels,
but do not have LOVE,
I am only a resounding gong or a clanging cymbal.

If I have the gift of prophecy and can fathom
all mysteries and all knowledge,
and if I have a faith that can move mountains,
but do not have LOVE, I am nothing.

If I give all I possess to the poor and give over my body
to hardship that I may boast,
but do not have LOVE, I gain nothing.

LOVE is patient, LOVE is kind. It does not envy,
it does not boast, it is not proud.

It does not dishonor others, it is not self-seeking,
it is not easily angered, it keeps no record of wrongs.
LOVE does not delight in evil but rejoices with the truth.

It always protects, always trusts, always hopes,
always perseveres.

LOVE never fails.
But where there are prophecies, they will cease;
where there are tongues, they will be stilled;
where there is knowledge, it will pass away.

For we know in part and we prophesy in part,
but when completeness comes,
what is in part disappears.

When I was a child, I talked like a child,
I thought like a child, I reasoned like a child.
When I became a man, I put the ways of childhood behind me.

For now we see only a reflection as in a mirror;
then we shall see face to face.
Now I know in part; then I shall know fully,
even as I am fully known.

And now these three remain: faith, hope, and love.
But the greatest of these is LOVE.

Gratefully,

John Delameter

Acknowledgements

There are so many people I want to thank for helping me bring this dream into reality. I never would have imagined about eight years ago that I'd still be alive today, never mind a published (and soon to be famous) author!

My heart is so full of gratitude and love for the experience.

This book would go on for several more chapters if I tried to name you all, so for now I'll have to stick to those who were significant influences and played major roles in the course of my life.

The listing here is random, so no nasty emails please about the order in which you appear, or if your name is not here at all!

So here we go...

To Bill Hodges:
Thank you for always being there for me, and especially that chilly day when I was planting bulbs in March (I still get teased about that!). We were both at a loss for words but your presence that day, and every day since, was a great comfort to me. I also want to thank you for encouraging me to find a professional writer to help me write the book, and for your constant advice and encouragement along the way.

To Richard Fawcett:
The whole idea to write a book about my life was birthed at your book study discussion group held on Saturday mornings at Unity Temple on the Plaza in Kansas City.

Richard, thank you for encouraging me to share my story with the group. At first, I was very reluctant to do so, but I trusted you enough to know you were always trying to lead me to my highest and greatest good. You were the first and only person that came to mind for the Dedication, and I hope you know just how much I love and appreciate you!

To Bambi Shen:
After I finished sharing my story at the book study discussion group, one of the other people in the class—Bambi Shen—who was very well-known around town and an author as well, turned to me and said, in her cute Vietnamese accent, "Why you not write book?" My response was, "I don't know how" and "I can't do that." And you replied, "I help."

I'm sorry that you passed away before we could move forward with anything, but know that from wherever you are, you're smiling and saying how proud you are of me! Rest in peace, dear Bambi.

To Mom and Pop:
Thank you for giving us life and thank you for making it a good one! You taught us courage, strong work ethics, how to help others, and the importance of never giving up. And the sense of humor you passed along to us was so dry, we always joked that it was a fire hazard!

Even though we had our challenges when I was growing up, as all families do, I know that you loved and always wanted the best for me. You weren't physically here to watch me raise a family, enjoy a long professional career, play with my grandchildren, or become the real man—a gay man—I was born to be. But I know you are and continue to watch over me with so much love and acceptance, from wherever you are, every step of the way. I miss you, love you, and thank you!

To my siblings:
I still say that growing up we were "One tent short of a full-blown circus!" But you all were always *MY* circus and boy did we have some crazy times over the years! But I honestly wouldn't change a thing.

To those of you still with us—Lea, Derald, Twylia, and Jo—I'm grateful to each of you for helping me throughout this book writing process.

Special thanks to Lea and Derald for being our family historians and helping me fill in the blanks in some of our family stories.

Twylia, thank you for continuing to be "the leader in the pack!" Sharing your experiences, strength, and hope, and guiding me in using the 12-Step recovery principles has helped me get through a lot.

And Jo, you are such a wiz at the spelling of family names, small details, and passing the word about this book!

H.A., George, Clay, Foster, Lillian, and Jerrie - I miss you but know you're proud of me and rooting for me from the great beyond! And thank you again, H.A., for writing *your* book all those years ago, which I was able to refer to from time to time.

To all of my siblings, thank you for influencing my life— sometimes for the better, sometimes for the worse—and I long for the day when we'll all be together again.

To Eva:
Our kids have become very loving, giving, and strong adults, and are both still very grounded in their faith.

Beth is busy being a wife and mom, loves scrapbooking, and is very active with the Normal Park and Recreation summer theater programs, as well as in her family's church. Brian, continues to enjoy his long career at State Farm and his new motorcycle.

David still enjoys being a father, his long career with the Ford Motor Company, and playing guitar.

Our grandchildren are doing amazing things as well:
Lynna is now married and working on pursuing a graduate degree in Chicago.

Mikey is also married, recently graduated from Middle Tennessee State University, and enjoys her work at a nonprofit organization.

Recently engaged, Ian is enrolled in Heartland Community College with a major in criminal justice and plans to marry in April of 2021.

Levi a senior in high school where he is a bass drummer, still enjoys the theater and has plans for a career in it.

Robby loves working as a stage sound and lighting tech, and is also busy composing, writing, and producing some pretty nice sounding music.

Nick is now living in Springfield, working, and doing well as an artist.

And Cody is happily married and has three kids, which makes you a Great Grandma!

Eva, you really did give me the best years of your life and I tried to give you mine. Thank you, again, for all you meant to me over the years, and for all that you will continue to mean to me from the other side.

Rest in peace, sweet lady.

To Anna Lea and Edward Streett:
Thank you for being wonderful in-laws and for openly accepting me as a part of your family. It still warms my heart when I think about how for years after Eva and I divorced, and you found out about my past, you still continued to call me your son. Rest in peace, dear ones.

To my children, Beth Briggs and David Delameter:
Beth and David, you are my heart and always will be. Thank you for allowing me to be your dad and for continuing to love and support me, even when my coming out was so hard on you. I never meant to cause you any pain, but I had to be myself and when it really counted you were always there for me – even if you didn't know what to say or how to feel.

Watching you grow up was one of the greatest joys (and challenges) in my life, and I learned to be more appreciative of my parents and the decisions they made when raising me. Because of you I also have a better understanding of God as my heavenly parent, and all that goes into raising me to be and live my best life.

Your love and encouragement during the writing of this book mean the world to me, and I'm so proud of the woman, man, and parents you have become!

To Brian, my son-in-law, and Jennifer, my former daughter-in-law:
Thank you for bringing your unique and individual beliefs and perspectives on life into our family. Although at times there were very different from what we believed, they still helped create an environment where we learned to be more open and accepting of others and their viewpoints.

To the four teachers that had a huge impact on my life:

Jessie Nichols-Alley was one of my one-room schoolhouse teachers. Using a huge felt board, she had a wonderful way of teaching us character building and of making the Old Testament interesting, understandable, and come alive, which have been helpful to me throughout my life.

Elford Horn, our fantastic band director, taught us that when performing, whether on a stage or on the football field, we were always to look and sound our very best. Nothing less would do. I've tried my best to follow this guidance throughout my life and it has served me well.

Roger Bryan taught a number of classes at Princeton High School, but the one that really stands out to me was an advanced business class my senior year. In it we learned how to apply for work, and then after we got a job to be there when we were supposed to be there, and to do the job the way we were told to do it. That advice has stuck with me all of these years.

Lorene Clingingsmith was my typing and publications teacher at Princeton High School, and it was through her that I gained an interest in what turned out to be an over 40-year career in printing. Little did I know that I would be able to use all of those skills one day to communicate on a thing called a personal computer! One question she asked us many times over was, "If you don't have time to do it right, when will you find time to do it over?" Ever since then, whenever I was doing something at work, or engaged in a project like painting or gardening, that question would come to mind. It not only saved me a lot of time but reminded me that it was important to always put my best foot forward. And I've shared that wisdom with others over the years as well.

I thank and appreciate you all. You are greatly missed.

To Earlene Shandrew Klein:
I credit you for Eva and I being able to have our son, David, in our lives. If you'd hadn't told me back in high school that the company I wanted to work for in Kansas City was only hiring for about three months so they didn't have to pay unemployment benefits, we would have never thought about moving to Lincoln. Many years later, we were connected to an adoption agency that we would have otherwise not known anything about. David is a true gift, and so are you.

To my friends in Lincoln:
Pastor Dennis Wood and Pastor Dale Phillips from Southview Baptist Church, and Brett Yahn and Mike King from the Baptist Student Union on the campus of the University of Nebraska, thank you all for teaching me that a relationship with God is very personal and achievable; that God was not just one of those unreachable "I'm going to get you gods" but a very loving and accepting one.

Although you are no longer with us, I also want to thank you, Pastor Dennis, for our very long friendship over the years, and for the times when we, along with your beautiful wife Sandy, were able to reconnect and reminisce in-person and across the miles. Sandy and I will carry on that tradition!

To my 12-Step Brothers and Sisters:
Through you I learned that in my youth I had created a mistaken interpretation that the Baptist faith had a monopoly on heaven. In the 12-Step meetings, each of you openly shared your unique life paths and beliefs. And what I learned and came to appreciate was that regardless of our religious beliefs, race, sexual orientation, gender, and so on, we could each find a Higher Power that worked for *us*, as individuals. So thank you for opening my eyes to a different way of seeing things.

To the late Bill Garnett:
Thank you for introducing me to The Landmark Forum. Although I was resistant at first, partly because I had a lot of things going on in my life at that time and didn't want to add another "have to" to my list, there was something about your

commitment to attend your weekly meetings that spoke to me. It was an obvious priority that you'd made in your life and when I finally accepted your invitation, I knew it was one of the best decisions I'd made in mine. I only wish you could see me now.

To Ron and Kerry, my former partners:
Thank you for loving and putting up with me during my second childhood! You both taught me how to be an equal partner in a relationship, and I'm very grateful for that. Rest in peace, Ron.

To Dr. Joe Nadeau and Dr. Dustin Cates, former artistic directors of the Heartland Men's Chorus:
Both of you, in combination with many of the other members, taught me about the energy that flows between the audience and the chorus. Through you I learned that from curtain up to the final bow, that energy is like a growing relationship through which a lot of healing can take place. I was healed through our messages about acceptance, celebrating diversity, and creating change in the world, and I know that many others were too. Thank you both, and the entire chorus, for "Proudly Singing Out in Kansas City Since 1986."

To the Center for Spiritual Living Kansas City:
In my over three years at CSL, my heart has been opened, and continues to be opened, to loving myself and others unconditionally. The teachings deeply rooted in New Thought principles and how to live in the present moment, instead of dwelling on any perceived mistakes of the past or fears of the future, have really changed my life.

I no longer believe I have to plead, beg, or make promises to God. I just know that God's promise to always be there to love, support, and provide for me will never change. I often say, "Everything I need today is on its way," and I thank CSL for gently guiding me to choose what I believe in my heart to be true.

To Lysa Allman-Baldwin:
Thank you for loving, supporting, and helping me write this book! I never realized how much goes into it and I really appreciate your professionalism, keeping me on track, and for combating my gift for misspelling and mispronunciation! There were so many emotional areas of my life that I got into and couldn't find the way through on my own, so I appreciate your guidance in leading me to make the book flow more smoothly. The thing that I'm most touched by is that I could trust you with things that up until we started working together, I'd never told anyone else. And no matter what it was, you listened with love and acceptance and helped me put it in just the right place to help make my story flow smoothly. I'm sure this book is going to be a great success because of all the hard work you put into it!

And last but certainly not least,
to my hometown of Princeton:

I couldn't think of a better place to grow up than Princeton, MO! It's where generations of my family were born, lived, worked, raised families, established businesses, retired, and made incredible contributions to the community and region at-large. My upbringing, in many ways, was the typical small-town life.

Everyone has different childhood experiences, whether they came from a small rural community, a big urban city, or somewhere in between. Neither one is better than the other—just different.

However, for me, starting my life in a close-knit community and later moving to bigger cities, has given me, shall we say, "a bookends perspective" that has really made an impact on my life. And I wouldn't change a thing.

Yes, growing up in a small Midwestern town in the 1940s and '50s had it challenges. And as you've read, I've had quite a few misgivings about how people thought and behaved around certain issues and lifestyles. But just like anything else, things evolve. People change their thinking. New ideas and ways of being come to the forefront. Life goes on and we all play a part in how we want to show up for those experiences. What I've noticed about my beloved Princeton during some of my recent visits back home is how much the social, political, and spiritual landscapes have changed.

242

All types of new business concepts are opening up. There is a strong focus on shopping local.

A new ministerial alliance has formed, bringing together churches and people of all faiths. And there seems to be a more open acceptance of people regardless of race, gender, sexual orientation, and religious beliefs.

During the COVID-19 pandemic, people continued to do whatever they could to support each other.

When a devastating fire destroyed the homes of over 30 people, the town didn't hesitate to come together to provide food, temporary housing, furniture, clothing, or raise money to help those who were affected.

And when Eva passed you showed me, my kids, and her family you were there for us with so much love and support.

It's that kind of thing that I experienced growing up here— people helping people.

That spirit of unity, oneness, and coming together has grown over the years and it makes me so proud to say Princeton is my hometown.

To everyone reading this, from near and far, I thank you all from the bottom of my heart.

With love, John

As a perfect child of God, I do not inherit sickness.
~ Myrtle Fillmore, co-founder of Unity

Fear is just a negative thought. Where is it showing up in your life?

Made in the USA
Middletown, DE
30 October 2020